CAN YOU HAVE TOO MUCH SEX?

CAN YOU HAVE TOO MUCH SEX?

APANDISIS
PUBLISHING

Apandisis Publishing
105 Madison Avenue, Suite 3A
New York, New York 10016

ISBN-13: 978-1-4127-5278-7
ISBN-10: 1-4127-5278-7

Manufactured in USA

8 7 6 5 4 3 2 1

www.FYIanswers.com

Contents

Chapter Three
HEALTH MATTERS

Chapter Six
ANIMAL KINGDOM

Chapter Seven
HISTORY

Chapter Eight
BODY SCIENCE

Chapter Nine
SPORTS

Chapter Ten
PEOPLE

Chapter One

LOVE AND LUST

Q Can you have too much sex?

A It depends on whom you ask. Your mother might tell you that too much of a good thing is bad, and a practitioner of Western medicine might agree.

Why? Imagine jumping a motorcycle over a car—it would be a real rush. But if you were to jump a motorcycle over that same car every day for a week, it would become less challenging and, thus, boring. Your brain would become accustomed to the feeling it received from those first jumps. To replicate the original thrill, you would need to up the ante. You would have to add another car to the line each day, and eventually you would suffer an injury.

How, you ask, does motorcycle jumping relate to sex? When you have sex, your body releases endorphins and a combination of neurostimulating chemicals, including dopamine, norepinephrine, oxytocin, and serotonin. Some Western doctors believe that with frequent sex, your brain eventually gets soaked in these chemicals. Ultimately, nothing is thrilling—and you go to unhealthy extremes as you try to recapture the feeling you experienced early on.

However, if you were to consult an Eastern practitioner of Tantra, a Taoist, a Hindu, or perhaps a Yogi, you might receive a different type of answer. These people might tell you that sex is something you can bring into every aspect of your life, and that making love is a practice that can take more than twelve hours, if it's done with the proper intention. For these folks, sex is not merely the insertion of part A into part B, followed by some vigorous agitation and spontaneous ejaculation. Sex is a way of expanding your connection with another person and with the universe at large, creating a harmonious whole.

These Eastern philosophers believe sex has roots in yoga, as it deals with releasing energy through the many *chakras*, or energy centers, of the body. An orgasm is not the goal—instead, sex focuses on enlightenment and understanding. And one can never be too enlightened, right?

Q Have astronauts had sex in space?

A Hitting golf balls on the moon and growing plants on a space station are cool things, but we amateur scientists at F.Y.I.

headquarters have a far more fascinating experiment in mind: Why not try for an orbital orgasm?

NASA claims that it's never happened, at least to the best of its knowledge, and the Russians aren't fessin' up, either. But rumors of astronauts secretly joining the two-hundred-mile-high club persist. The most likely space lovers were newlywed astronauts Mark Lee and Jan Davis, who went on a mission together in 1992. The couple, however, declined to comment on any possible amorous encounters. Gossip has also centered on two flirty Russians who shared close quarters on the Mir space station in the 1990s, but there's no evidence of a celestial booty call.

Could it happen? It's doubtful on the Space Shuttle, where there's almost no privacy. On the International Space Station, however, it would be possible to sneak away for some nookie. But even there, the circumstances wouldn't exactly be ideal.

Take it from NASA physician Jim Logan, who outlined several potential obstacles to outer-space intercourse at the Space Frontier Foundation's NewSpace conference in 2006:

Without gravity's help, getting it on would be a burdensome task—a true space oddity. For starters, you'd probably have to strap yourself to your partner and to the wall (though that might appeal to the kinky crowd).

The potential glitches don't end there. It might also get too hot and sweaty for most people—in microgravity, you tend to sweat more, and there's no convection to dissipate body heat. Then there are the fluids associated with sex, which form floating droplets and—well, you get the idea. Finally, the drop in blood pressure that people experience in outer space would shrink an important piece of a man's lovemaking equipment.

No, the picture isn't pretty—but who could resist the chance to be the first? It would be one quickie for man (and woman), one giant score for mankind.

Q Why don't guys wear engagement rings?

A Hey, who says the guys can't show off a little bling, too? In parts of Germany, Scandinavia, and the Basque regions of Spain, both spouses-to-be begin wearing gold bands once they get engaged. The practice is becoming more customary in the United Kingdom and the United States, too. No longer will she appear to be taken while he roams the bars ambiguously unmarked and free.

Things sure have come a long way since the days of the original engagement rings. According to some jewelry historians, these were reeds and rushes that early men procured to literally bind and claim their mates. But the Neanderthal wasn't a total caveman. When he was certain his captive love wouldn't run away, he did minimize her bindings to a single loop that fit right around her finger. Isn't that romantic?

Good thing Archduke Maximilian of Austria knew a little better. It's believed that he was the first man to present a diamond engagement ring to his betrothed when he gave one to Mary of Burgundy in 1477. Over time (and several brilliant marketing campaigns by De Beers in the mid-twentieth century), the sparkly solitaire became an essential, loud-and-clear signal of a woman's spoken-for status—and her future husband's ability to provide for her. (Perhaps you've heard that a guy is supposed to propose with a ring that's worth two to three months of his salary?)

But modern times have brought men and women closer to equal positions in the workplace, at home, and in love. This means that most women are no longer waiting around for a man to come along and tie her up with wild cattails. Nowadays, the number of women doing the proposing is on the rise, so the demand for male engagement rings is also up. Tradition holds that you seal the deal with something bright and shiny, after all.

Okay, most men don't spend their days dreaming of flawless, three-carat, pear-shaped diamonds that are set in platinum. So engagement rings for men are typically simple gold or titanium bands with more discreet, inset stones. A spokesperson for the H. Samuel jewelry chain in the United Kingdom says, "The men's engagement ring is a clear message to everyone that a man is going to be married and also works perfectly for civil partnerships."

But listen up, guys: If your ladylove (or gentleman love) pops the question and presents you with a ring, just be aware of the specific etiquette involved in showcasing the thing. A bride wears her wedding and engagement rings on the same finger, but a man doesn't. The male engagement ring is worn on the ring finger of the left hand up until the wedding. After that, the engagement ring moves to the ring finger of the right hand and the wedding band is worn on the left.

It's a look that Liberace would have loved.

Q Do they have orgies at nudist resorts?

A To the average sexually repressed American, a nudist resort seems like a fantasyland: calendar-worthy men and women playing beach volleyball all day long and then retiring to the pool bar for mai tais and wild, uninhibited lovemaking. But anybody who visits one of these resorts expecting to hook up with sexy Playboy bunnies is sorely mistaken. You're more likely to come across sexagenarians wearing floppy beach hats (with the hats probably being the least floppy thing about them). Furthermore, the idea that nudist resorts are dens of hedonistic orgies is, for the most part, a misconception born of the typical person's misunderstanding of nudism.

Nudism isn't just about getting naked in front of other people. It's rooted in a philosophy—or, at least, the original movement was. Nudism, or naturism, as it is also called, dates to ancient times, when Indian ascetics practiced it as a way to symbolize the eschewing of worldly possessions. But nudism as a modern social movement didn't really start until the late nineteenth century; perhaps in response to the dehumanizing effects of the Industrial Revolution and the prudery of the Victorian era, social thinkers promoted it as a way to be more ecologically aware and to encourage equality among the classes. This led to large naturist movements in Germany and England, which soon spread across the pond to the United States.

Nowadays, there are dozens of nudist resorts around the United States. They work pretty much like your average holiday resort—except, of course, visitors don't wear any clothes. But the proprietors of these resorts, as well as organizational bodies promoting nudism (such as the International Naturist Federation), go to great pains to underscore that orgies are not a common practice at nudist resorts. Indeed, many naturist thinkers insist that sexuality and eroticism have no place in the nudist philosophy whatsoever and that nudism is a moral and safe practice that even families can practice together. (Um, no thanks.)

However, this doesn't mean that *all* nudist resorts don't allow orgies. A resort in tropical North Queensland, Australia, known as the White Cockatoo recently established an "almost anything goes" policy for the month of March. Though White Cockatoo proprietors didn't explicitly state that wild orgies would be the norm, they claimed that "it doesn't take rocket science" to get their meaning.

Now please excuse us while we go book a flight to Australia.

Q Can an alpha male and an alpha female get along?

A They sure can—just like two obnoxiously overachieving peas in a pod.

The term "alpha" is borrowed from the study of animal behavior, where it refers to the dominant member of a social group of animals. Among humans, it refers to those successful, wealthy, good-looking people who seem to be able to keep more plates spinning than the rest of us. They tend to be well educated, and when they aren't in their corner offices making executive decisions, they're out in the community volunteering, serving on boards and com-

missions, and coaching in youth sports leagues. They have thousands of friends, they're fit and trim, and their skin looks fabulous.

In the past, we most often associated these alpha characteristics with men. The stereotypical alpha male chose a mate based on her looks, her age, and her inability or lack of desire to challenge his authority. She was often called a trophy wife—especially if she wasn't his first wife—and she was certainly no alpha herself.

But the times have changed. Females have gained a foothold in the workplace; meanwhile, ever more women have had to be the heads of their single-parent households. The image of the alpha female has taken shape: She's in control and doesn't need a man.

According to a 2004 article in *Psychology Today* called "The New Trophy Wife," these alphas are more often seeking other alphas when it comes time to settle down. Alpha males, the article asserts, are shifting their amorous gazes toward women who are more like themselves: accomplished go-getters rather than beautiful doormats.

The potential reasons are varied. One explanation is that an alpha male who chooses a traditional trophy wife is now seen as weak by his peers—he's afraid of the challenge presented by a strong woman. Another theory is that men who were raised by single mothers are less threatened by female power. They've never lived with submissive, June Cleaver types and, consequently, don't expect these sorts of companions in relationships.

Meanwhile, an alpha female finds that she is attracted to a man who can hold up his end of the bargain in an overachieving partnership. But Dr. Pam Spurr, a British psychologist and sex expert, insists that even in these alpha-on-alpha relationships, some traditional gender roles still exist. "What I've found about many alpha women is that in reality, they do want a really powerful man in their lives, but perhaps they think it's horribly old-fashioned to admit the fact," Spurr says. "The element of the alpha woman's character most deeply hidden is that secretly she longs to be taken care of."

So maybe it's just a matter of degrees. Although we mere mortals can't see it, even in the rarefied air of peaceful alphahood, the alpha male is still the true alpha.

Q Can a man increase his penis size?

A When seeking the answers to life's most important questions, we here at F.Y.I. headquarters seek out the wise counsel of the world's most accurate source: the spam folder of our in-box. *So, let's see here...log on to the email account...check out the spam folder.*

Wow! There are 684 messages—we sure are popular. And even more exciting, it appears that there *are* ways to increase penis size. At least 684 of them, including several "ancient Arab" techniques, a few "secrets of the Orient," and assorted patches, pills, pumps, and powders. Next question, please.

Okay, so our bosses just told us that the spam folder isn't a reliable source. Nevertheless, the vast number of penis-enhancement advertisements clogging the Internet shows that this is a topic that preoccupies men. For thousands of years, in fact, quacks and snake-oil salesmen—history's equivalent of email spammers—have made penis-enlargement promises that they couldn't keep. The main techniques hawked over the centuries have been pills, pumps, exercises, and surgery.

Let's start with herbal supplements, which currently are a popular enhancement option. The National Center for Complementary and Alternative Medicine found that herbal pills may help with certain conditions, but a lilliputian penis isn't among them. There is no evidence that the millions of dollars men spend each year on penis enlargement pills are doing any good whatsoever.

Pumps are another hot product on the penis front. They work to stimulate blood flow to the penis, inducing erections in men with erectile dysfunction disorder. They can add size temporarily (due to the increased blood flow), but that's about it. Pumps have no long-term impact on penis size—in fact, they may cause injury if they're overused or used improperly.

In these plastic-surgery-obsessed times, it shouldn't come as a surprise that penis-enhancement procedures are another big business. But unlike the quackery we mentioned earlier, there is some evidence that surgical techniques can *indeed* increase penis size. Nevertheless, surgery is a hotly debated—and a largely unregulated—technique.

A couple different types of surgery are available. The first involves injecting the patient's own fat into the penis. Problem is, the surgery can lead to infection and scarring; worse, it can leave the penis appearing fatty and lumpy, like a hot dog that's been cooked too long in the microwave.

The second, and more popular, technique involves cutting the ligament that helps suspend the penis from the pubic bone and then surgically adding skin in order to bridge the newly added length. The result is that the penis hangs down farther. According to the few studies that have been conducted on this procedure, men can add an average of a quarter-inch to a flaccid penis. Hey, that's better than nothing, right?

Maybe not. Doctors have recorded instances of the man's penis shrinking following this type of surgery, because the ligament spontaneously reattached itself to the pubic bone. That isn't exactly an ideal result—especially since the cost, up to ten thousand dollars (excluding additional corrective surgery if it's required), probably won't be covered by insurance because it's a cosmetic procedure. The whole thing can be a dismaying case of subtraction by addition.

Ironically, penis size shouldn't even be an issue for men. The average penis is between three and four inches long while flaccid and around five to seven inches long while erect, and numerous surveys suggest that the vast majority of women are perfectly happy with these measurements.

The message? Men simply need to learn how to better use the equipment they have. And if that fails, they can always buy a bigger SUV.

Q When are you allowed to get an annulment instead of a divorce?

A Annulments are further proof that breaking up is hard to do. As with the relationships that precede them, annulments can be complicated. So let's start from square one. There are two types of annulment: religious and secular.

First, the religious. The Roman Catholic Church will annul a marriage if it finds that the union doesn't meet the standards of matrimony as defined by the Catechism of the Catholic Church. Unlike divorce, which the church doesn't recognize, an annulment isn't a dissolution of marriage—it's a declaration that there was no marriage in the first place. The church recognizes several criteria for annulment, which are broken down into three categories.

A marriage may be annulled because of a "lack of canonical form," meaning that it occurred outside the laws of the church. If, for example, you were married in a civil ceremony without any approval from the church, you can get an annulment. The next category is "impediments to marriage," in which the couple wasn't eligible to be married. Let's say the two are close relatives or are underage—the marriage doesn't count.

Finally, there is "defect of consent." This is the most common type of religious annulment, covering situations in which either person takes his or her vows for reasons other than a wholehearted desire to do so. For example, if a pregnant bride's parents pressure her into marrying the baby's father, there are clear grounds for annulment. Defect of consent also applies to scenarios in which one person deceived the other about something (homosexuality, for example). Additionally, it takes into account the couple's psychological state, including immaturity. If either person wasn't thinking rationally when the marital deed was done, the couple could have grounds for an annulment.

Onward to the secular front. A civil annulment is a legal recognition that a marriage never took place because it didn't meet the standards of a valid union. The details vary by state but follow similar criteria. If either person is already married or underage (the exact age varies by state), or if the couple is closely related (the definition varies by state), the marriage is considered a "void marriage," or one that was invalid in the first place.

A marriage is also voidable if any of the following can be demonstrated: One person didn't have the mental capacity to decide to wed; the marriage was based on fraud, deception, or force; one person was impotent or had a venereal disease and didn't disclose it to the other; or the couple got married as a joke and had no intention of staying wed. To void any of these types of marriages, you typically need to make your annulment request expediently; saying that you tied the knot as a joke two years after the fact probably isn't going to cut the legal mustard. So if you get drunk and marry a stranger who turns out to have herpes, don't procrastinate. Go down to the courthouse right away.

Q What do women want?

A It's one of the world's greatest mysteries, right up there with "How did the universe begin?" and "Where is Jimmy Hoffa's body?" The truth is, most men find women to be as confusing and complex as Fermat's last theorem (a math problem that confounded scholars for more than three hundred and fifty years).

Women—how can anyone even begin to explain them? They make next to no sense. Their MOs are top secret. They come from an entirely different planet and speak their own language (Venusian). Heck, even Sigmund Freud—one of the most authoritative thinkers of the twentieth century—couldn't figure them out. Before his death, the founder of psychoanalysis admitted: "The great question that has never been answered, and which I have not yet been able to answer, despite my thirty years of research into the feminine soul, is, 'What does a woman want?'"

Well, Siggy, maybe you were just delving a bit too deep into the female psyche. Penis envy—really? Guys, here's one thing you can be sure of: When it comes to what a woman wants, chances are that she does not long for her very own Mr. Happy. In reality, most women only want a few very simple things. Things like:

Appreciation. Adoration. R-E-S-P-E-C-T. A pair of jeans that fit. A husband who remembers anniversaries.

The power to crash through the glass ceiling. To call in sick on a bad hair day. Equal pay for equal work. A sugar daddy. Exactly 1.5 children—who can drive themselves to soccer practice.

Integrity. Honesty. To know where this relationship is going. Spontaneity. Surprises. Flowers for no reason at all—but not carnations, please.

A small green salad with fat-free ranch on the side. A tub of chocolate chip cookie dough with a spoon. A group of Cosmodrinking gal pals who will always be there for her. To be thinner and prettier than all of them.

Complete self-reliance and independence. Someone to open car doors and pickle jars, and kill household creepy-crawlies. A closet that can be walked into. Top-of-the-line cooking and cleaning appliances. A maid to do all of the dishes and laundry.

To be appreciated and admired for her intelligence. To look really hot in a mini skirt. Bigger breasts. Smaller thighs. To just be accepted for who she is.

Someone to sleep next to every night. Someone who does not burp, bleep, snore, toss, or turn. A good guy. A bad boy. A really sensual massage. To just be left the hell alone.

To have it all. To live simply. The option to change her mind about any or all of the above at any given moment without prior notice.

Now, what's so confusing about that?

Q What does sex have to do with the birds and the bees?

A Listen up, Dad: Chip is an adolescent now. A few years fraught with misery, self-consciousness, and an almost incomprehensible awkwardness lay ahead—and it'll be even worse for your kid. And you know that nothing will be more excruciating for either of you than the requisite "facts of life" talk. But for God's sake, man, don't make it any harder than it has to be by bumbling your way through a half-assed explanation about "the birds and the bees."

It's tempting to use the birds and the bees as a metaphor for sex. For the past couple hundred years or so, the term has been common shorthand for referring to the entirety of the natural kingdom. But only since the 1930s has it been definitively used to refer to sex. The origin of the phrase is up for debate: Some etymologists believe that it may have been inspired by a 1928 Cole Porter song, "Let's Do It," while others think it's rooted in something far older, Samuel Taylor Coleridge's 1825 poem "Work Without Hope."

Either way, it seems doubtful that the birds and the bees are a very good analogy for the human reproductive process. While birds and bees pollinate flowers, and the female reproductive parts of a flower are vaguely—superficially—similar to those of a human female, a cursory glance at the mating habits of birds and bees shows that these creatures have just about nothing to do with human sex. Unless you have a really weird fetish. In which case you probably shouldn't be talking to your children about sex at all.

Although the story of the birds and the bees has been a convenient way to talk about the reproductive process for several decades, it's pretty obvious that the whole metaphor is tenuous. Birds hatch from eggs, for cripes sakes—what exactly are you trying to teach your kids? And bees? Perhaps before suggesting that your child look to the mating behavior of bees as a guide to sexual behavior, you should consider this: Virtually all bees die as virgins. That's largely because, in a honeybee colony, all of the male bees fight to mate with a single female, the queen. Not many succeed. The reward for those who do? Castration and death. Welcome to the world of adult sex, kids!

So when it's finally time for the dreaded talk, treat your kids like the intelligent beings they are and leave out the birds and the bees. On second thought, there might not be a need for the talk at all. As Internet-savvy as kids are these days, your child probably knows more about sex than you do.

Q How long do sperm live after ejaculation?

A Like any other cell, sperm survive by absorbing nutrients and converting them into energy that powers everything they do. The difference, of course, is that sperm cells have to do their jobs outside the body, where there is neither a constant nutrient supply nor an optimal environment for survival. Their time on the outside is limited.

To give a sperm a fighting chance on its difficult journey, the male body packs a sack lunch of sorts. Sperm make up 2 to 5 percent of a brew called semen; the rest is seminal plasma, which includes nutrients to give the sperm energy and chemicals to neutralize the mildly acidic environment of the vagina. But even with these supplies, the going gets tough for sperm that are inside a woman's body. About 30 percent of the two hundred million to three hundred million sperm in a typical ejaculation are dead or defective right off the bat. And the clock is ticking for the rest, since they have limited amounts of energy to propel them on their all-important mission.

Sperm can survive in the vagina for only about six hours. But for sperm that make it past the vagina and into the cervix, life expectancy is up to eight days. These sperm hang out in mucus-lined folds in the cervix that are called crypts, which provide a waiting area before the journey continues to the less-hospitable uterus. The sperm enter the uterus in shifts rather than all at once; this orderly procession increases the chances that at least some will be in the right place when an ovum (egg) finally arrives. Only a few hundred sperm even make it far enough to take their shots at fertilizing the egg.

The outlook is grim for sperm that, for whatever reasons, never make it into the vagina. Outside the body, semen dries to the point that all of the sperm will die, often within minutes and certainly within hours. What's a poor little sperm to do? Wind up in a sperm bank, where the semen is specially frozen. Those puppies can live for years.

Q Why do some Mormons practice polygamy?

A Because a guy named Joseph Smith told them that they could. Like many other tenets of the Mormon faith, the one-time acceptance of polygamy—which has long been repudiated by the mainline Mormon church—came from Smith's revelations.

Smith, born in 1805 in Vermont, claimed that his first divine encounter occurred when he was fourteen. It happened when he was walking, deep in thought, in the woods of upstate New York, where his family had moved shortly after his birth. He was trying to determine which variation of Christianity was correct. Luckily for Smith, his confusion was put to rest when two figures appeared—God and Jesus Christ—and told him that all of the established churches had it wrong.

Four years later, an angel named Moroni told him about a set of golden plates that were inscribed in a mysterious language and were buried in the local hills. Another four years passed before Moroni allowed him to excavate these plates and gave him a set of stones that empowered him to translate them. (Unfortunately for posterity, Moroni wanted the plates back before they could be studied by less sympathetic observers.) The plates detailed the story of a tribe of Israelites that traveled to America thousands of years ago and was visited by Jesus after the resurrection.

In 1830, Smith published his translation as the *Book of Mormon* and founded a new church, the Church of Christ. One of the core beliefs, then and now, is that God was once like a man and became divine after progressing through lives in several celestial realms. Mormons hold that, in the fullness of time, anybody can become like God by following the right path.

The *Book of Mormon* explicitly forbids polygamy. But evidence suggests that as early as 1833, Smith and some of the other church elders were practicing plural marriage in secret. Smith himself may have had thirty or more wives. Of course, it's not easy to keep such a well-stocked harem under wraps; the Mormon community was widely suspected of sanctioning polygamy, which was one of the reasons that Mormons were persecuted wherever they went. Things came to a head in 1844 when Joseph Smith was murdered by an angry mob.

After Smith's death, Brigham Young became the head of the church. In 1847, he led his followers west to escape persecution.

They settled on land that would soon become the Utah Territory. There, separated from their persecutors and enjoying the wide-open freedoms of the Western frontier, the Mormon community finally admitted what had long been known: Brigham Young revealed in 1852 that many Mormons lived in polygamy. He said that Smith had been given a revelation in 1843 that condoned plural marriage. According to Young, Smith's first wife, Emma, had destroyed Smith's handwritten account of this divine message. (For her part, Emma claimed that Brigham Young had fabricated the entire story.)

Thus began the golden age of Mormon polygamy. The church encouraged the practice to such an extent that Brigham Young said in 1866, "The only men who become gods, even the Sons of God, are those who enter into polygamy." The U.S. government was less than thrilled with this flouting of conventional morality and exerted whatever pressure it could to force the Mormons to end their polygamous practices.

This conflict culminated with laws in 1887 that allowed the government to seize the property of polygamous Mormons. By this time, Young was long dead and the church had become more conciliatory. The law was upheld by the Supreme Court in 1890, and soon afterward the church's president at the time, Wilford Woodruff, announced a new revelation: Polygamy would no longer be allowed.

Since then, the largest Mormon church—the Church of Jesus Christ of Latter-day Saints—has disavowed polygamy. However, small numbers of Mormons have formed splinter sects that have continued the practice in order to progress toward godhood as

Smith and Young had instructed. According to some estimates, there are as many as a hundred thousand people who live in plural marriages in the name of Mormon beliefs—and in defiance of the law.

Q Why are women called the fairer sex?

A "The female body is a work of art," Elaine says in an episode of *Seinfeld*. "The male body is utilitarian; it's for gettin' around, like a jeep." When Jerry asks her if she finds the male body unattractive, Elaine admits, "It's hideous. The hair, the lumpiness—it's simian." There's no getting around it: If art museums and beer commercials—and sitcoms, of course—are any indication, the female form is the one we think is fairer.

Nobody knows the origin of the phrase "the fairer sex," but recent scientific research indicates that whoever coined it was right on the money. Even when we consider meanings of "fair" beyond "pretty" or "attractive," it seems that women have cornered the market.

Think about your typical Hollywood love story. When the hunky male lead finally sweeps the swooning ingénue off her feet and gives her that first long romantic kiss, note the difference in the skin tones of their faces: The man is invariably darker than the woman. Filmmakers have always known what science is now confirming: From adolescence on, a woman's complexion is lighter than a man's. It's true in many different populations around the world, and it can be explained by the fact that women have more subcutaneous fat (that is, fat directly beneath the skin). This fat protects the skin from the sex hormones that increase pigmentation, keeping women's skin fairer than men's.

But let's take it one step further. Women may also be fairer in another sense. A policy research report prepared for the World Bank in 1999 suggests that the presence of women in governments may make those ruling bodies more equitable. In "Are Women Really the 'Fairer' Sex? Corruption and Women in Government," economists David Dollar (a guy born to work for the World Bank), Raymond Fisman, and Roberta Gatti point to a growing body of research demonstrating that women are less selfish and more ethical than men.

Armed with this data, they took standardized ratings of government corruption around the world and compared them to the numbers of women participating in those governments. They found that the more women were involved in a government, the better its score tended to be on the corruption scale.

We won't argue with science, but we have our own, simpler theory about why women are called the fairer sex: They're soft and they smell good.

Q Do cold showers really work?

A Well, what do you want them to do for you? In their book *Health$_2$O*, Dr. Alexa Fleckenstein and Roanne Weisman claim that cold showers and other cold-water therapies can work all sorts of health wonders, including boosting the immune system, fighting off colds and the flu, increasing blood flow to the organs, and teaching the body to keep itself warmer in cold weather.

Or maybe you want to live to be one hundred? Centenarian Edward Rondthaler of Croton-on-Hudson, New York, told CNN in 2006 that he attributed his longevity to, among other things, regular cold showers. Rondthaler said that since 1918, he had ended his showers every morning by switching the water from hot to cold and counting to one hundred.

But let's stop being coy and address the real issue implied in the question: Will a cold shower put the brakes on a turbocharged sex drive? One study conducted in the United Kingdom found quite the opposite effect. When doctors at the Thrombosis Research Institute in London asked approximately two hundred people to take regular cold baths for a year, they observed that men in the study had increased levels of testosterone—cold baths actually boosted their libidos. Dr. Vijay Kakkar, who heads up the institute, was not surprised by the results. Kakkar observed that in his native India, cold baths have been recommended for centuries as a way to improve a person's sex life.

But even that doesn't really answer the question, does it? We're talking about something much more simple and direct: spraying some horny bastard with cold water. Will it have a temporary effect? Everybody thinks it does, but there doesn't seem to be a pressing desire in the scientific community to prove it, so there's no body of evidence.

Here's what we suggest: Try it yourself. (All in the name of science, of course.) Find a willing partner, get your thang goin' on, and then toss off your lab coats and jump into a cold shower and see what happens. Nobody's ever going to confuse the F.Y.I. staff with Masters and Johnson or Dr. Ruth Westheimer, but we're guessing that your evening of fun in the lab won't end there.

Q Is penis envy for real?

A Normally, this is where we make a sophomoric joke about male genitalia and feelings of inadequacy. But since we have reams of material to condense into a handful of paragraphs, we're going to forgo the comedy layups and head straight to the heart of the matter.

The term "penis envy" was coined by the founder of psychoanalysis, Sigmund Freud. If you know anything about Freud's works, you can probably guess that the answer to this question is going to delve into dark and disturbing territory. Freud was one of the first people to speculate about our unconscious mind; according to his tug-of-war theory of personality, the conscious mind is constantly trying to subjugate the desires of the unconscious mind.

Many of Freud's ideas have come under fire from contemporary psychologists, and none is more controversial than his notion of penis envy. We're talking about the craziest idea from a guy who was known for crazy ideas.

In broad terms, Freud's theory states that each child goes through a series of psychosexual stages that lead to healthy adult sexuality, provided they're dealt with correctly. These stages, from first to last, are: oral, anal, phallic, latency, and genital. Freud claimed that in the phallic stage, children of both sexes begin to develop a sexual attraction toward the mother. While this attachment may be unconscious, Freud argued that it is very real and a powerful element in the child's burgeoning personality.

This part of Freud's theory might ring a bell: The desire to possess one parent while, by necessity, replacing the other is known as the infamous Oedipal complex (named after the character Oedipus from Greek mythology who unknowingly kills his father and marries his mother). As if this weren't upsetting enough, Freud believed that the real crisis comes when the child realizes that he or she can't compete with the stronger, smarter parent. The manner in which the child deals with this conundrum can radically affect his or her behavior in adulthood.

Naturally, gender is an important component here. For a little girl, this Oedipal crisis is called the Electra complex and is exacerbated by the realization that she can never have a sexual relationship with her mother because she is lacking a penis. And there you have it: penis envy.

Think about this (if you dare). You're a young girl, you want to have sex with your mother, but you have no penis: What are you going to do? Well, according to Freud, you push your mother away, and your sexual fixation migrates to your father and *his* penis! As a result, the girl begins to emulate her mother in an effort to be more attractive to her father and, thus, she begins to inhabit her "appropriate" sexual role. According to Freud, anyway. We don't want to take any of the heat for this theory because it only gets worse from here.

A healthy management of this period leads to sexual attraction to men other than the father and ultimately results in babies, minivans, and Sunday night dinners at Applebee's. But if a young girl gets hung up in this phallic phase of sexual development, she can have difficulty forming healthy romantic relationships later on; Freud, in an even stranger leap of logic, went as far as to suggest that this may be the root of homosexuality.

If all of this seems ludicrous to you, you're not alone. (This is, remember, one of Freud's most disputed theories.) Nevertheless, since we're talking about an abstract and unconscious psychological phenomenon, it's difficult to unequivocally say that the concept of penis envy is false. But we're going to do so anyway. Why? We'll all sleep better at night and feel more comfortable at Thanksgiving dinner.

Q What's so attractive about an hourglass figure?

A It's no secret that men's eyes tend to zero in on female figures that have ample hips and busts and itty-bitty waists. But it may be that the guys just can't help themselves.

According to evolutionary psychologists like Devendra Singh of the University of Texas at Austin, humans may be hardwired to prefer those curvy, Barbie-doll proportions. The "allure of the hourglass figure is evident across generations in ancient cultures," says Singh. But just what explains its universal and enduring appeal?

If the evolutionary psychologists are right, men have a built-in understanding that a woman's proportions offer some reliable clues about her reproductive potential. And what exactly is the hourglass shape telling a man? That this is one healthy, fertile chick.

Over the years, medical studies have concluded that women with waist-to-hip ratios (measured by dividing waist circumference by hip circumference) of 0.7 or lower have less difficulty conceiving children and lower rates of chronic disease. Not coincidentally, research has revealed that men seem to prefer a waist-to-hip ratio of 0.7 or lower when looking for a mate.

Our brains developed a preference for this trait because of its link to good health, Singh suggests. For proof, look just take a gander at the pages of *Playboy*. (It's all in the name of science, of course.) An analysis of the figures of *Playboy* centerfold models found that the majority of these women had waist-to-hip ratios of 0.7 or lower. If that doesn't seal the deal for you, consider this little nugget: Marilyn Monroe, widely considered to have the ideal hourglass figure, had measurements of 36–24–34, or that "magic" waist-to-hip ratio of 0.7.

Nevertheless, not all researchers buy into the theories of evolutionary psychology. In his book *Adapting Minds*, David Buller of

Northern Illinois University says that there is a possibility that the appeal of the hourglass figure is not actually innate—that it's just the result of mass media culture and the messages it sends about what constitutes beauty.

It seems that in isolated populations (where men don't have constant cable TV access to the bombshell bods of Rita Hayworth, Sophia Loren, and Scarlett Johansson), there is a very different view of what constitutes an attractive female figure. In fact, in Peru and Tanzania, men perceive women with hourglass figures to look rather sickly. Their preference? Women who have waist-to-hip ratios of 0.9—in other words, women who have a little more to love around the middle.

Chapter Two

WEIRD SCIENCE AND TECHNOLOGY

Q Can you really pick up radio stations on your dental work?

A If you've watched enough *Gilligan's Island,* you know that it can happen on TV. And maybe you've heard that it happened in real life to Lucille Ball of *I Love Lucy* fame. According to Jim Brochu, author of *Lucy in the Afternoon,* the actress claimed that her dental fillings picked up radio signals as she drove to her home outside Los Angeles in 1942. She also claimed that the signals

were later traced to a Japanese spy who was eventually taken into custody by law enforcement authorities, perhaps the FBI.

Who knows if Lucy's tale is true? Nobody's found documented evidence of a Japanese spy nest infiltrating California in 1942, and Lucy's FBI file contains no mention of such an event. (Yes, Lucy had an FBI file. At the urging of her grandfather, she had registered to vote as a Communist in the 1936 elections, so she had some 'splaining to do when she was investigated by the House Select Committee on Un-American Activities in 1953.) Recently, the Discovery Channel television show *MythBusters* devoted a segment to debunking Lucy's claims.

Other people have claimed that they picked up radio signals via the metal in their heads, whether it was dental work or something else. The anecdotal accounts are easy to find but hard to verify. In 1981, however, a doctor in Miami wrote to *The American Journal of Psychiatry* to report that he had treated a patient who suffered from headaches and depression and complained of hearing music and voices. The patient was a veteran who had been wounded by shrapnel to the head during combat twelve years earlier. But after receiving successful treatment for the headaches and depression, the patient claimed that he still heard the mental music.

This led the doctor to sit down with the patient and a radio; the two of them listened to various stations, trying to find one that matched what the patient heard in his head. When they found what seemed to be the offending frequency, the doctor listened to the radio with an earphone while the patient described what he was hearing in his head. Although the patient couldn't hear the voices clearly, he passed the test convincingly; he was even able to tap out the rhythm and hum along with the songs that played.

The doctor concluded that the shrapnel in this man's head was receiving radio signals and conducting the sound through bone to his ear.

So apparently, it is possible for the metal in your head to receive radio transmissions—but don't look for the American Dental Association to begin marketing the iTooth portable music player anytime soon.

Q If you donate your body to science, what do they do with it?

A You can rest assured that scientists don't take donated cadavers out for wild *Weekend at Bernie's*-style partying or prop them in passenger seats just to use the carpool lanes. Typically, donating your body to science means willing it to a medical school, where it will be dissected to teach medical students about anatomy.

Fresh cadavers aren't as critical to medical schools as they once were, thanks to detailed models, computer simulations, and a better ability to preserve corpses. But they're still a much-appreciated learning aid. If you have a rare deformity or disease, your corpse will be especially useful.

Medical schools aren't allowed to buy bodies, rob graves, or go door to door recruiting volunteers, so they rely on potential donors to initiate contact. If you want to donate your body, you'll need to find a medical school in your area that has a body donation program. Your state's anatomical board is typically a good place to start. Once you've found a program, you fill out some legal paper-work and perhaps get a body donor identification card to carry in your wallet. Some schools will cover the cost of transporting your corpse to the school, within a certain distance, as well as crema-tion costs; others won't pay for transportation.

This is very different from organ donation, which you can arrange in many states by adding a note to your driver's license and shar-ing your wishes with your family. If you're an organ donor and die under the right circumstances (you're brain-dead but on a respi-rator), the doctors may extract your heart, kidneys, lungs, liver, pancreas, or small intestine and whisk the pieces to the organ recipients. But if you aren't on a respirator when you die, these internal organs won't be usable.

If you've already donated your organs, most medical schools won't accept what's left of your body. You're also out of luck if you died from a major trauma, had a contagious disease, or underwent major surgery within thirty days of your passing. And if you were obese or emaciated or your body has deteriorated? Again, you're out of luck.

Even when you're dead, it seems, getting into medical school is difficult.

Q Why does salt melt ice?

A The link between salt and hypertension is clear. Yet each winter highway departments dump billions of tons of salt onto the nation's frozen highways, with complete disregard for the health of the nation's transportation arteries. Is it any wonder that our highways are pitted with potholes? More importantly, has anybody considered the link between salt on the highways and the increase in incidents of road rage?

Until somebody tackles these really important questions, we'll have to satisfy ourselves with the explanation for why all that salt gets dumped in the first place. No, it's not to add a savory zing to the roads—it's to melt the ice. But in order to understand how salt melts ice, we'll need to take a trip back to chemistry class, where we learned how water freezes.

Water, as we all know, is known chemically as H_2O—it's two hydrogen atoms and one oxygen atom that bind together to form a molecule. These molecules are always bouncing about, though this movement is contingent on temperature. Heat speeds up the movement of molecules; cold slows it down. Eventually, if the temperature gets cold enough, water molecules cling together to form ice. As even we chemistry dummies know, this happens at thirty-two degrees Fahrenheit.

In order to melt ice, either the outside temperature needs to go up (a sunny day, for example) or the freezing point of the water itself must be lowered to below thirty-two degrees. Enter salt. When salt is dumped onto ice, the salt molecules bind with the water molecules; as a result, a colder temperature is required for the salt and water molecules to break apart so that ice can be formed.

However, this process requires that some water be present—if the temperature is too cold, there won't be any liquid water molecules to which the salt molecules can bind. (This is why in especially cold

climates, highway trucks sometimes dump sand onto roadways—
sand doesn't bind with water, but it does provide better traction.)

This principle is applied in other fields as well. In culinary school,
chefs are taught that adding salt to water raises the temperature
at which water boils, and the same idea is behind how antifreeze
keeps your engine from freezing or locking up in the winter.

It's tempting to think that this would work with the human body
as well: A couple of teaspoons of salt should warm you up, right?
We don't recommend it. Though salt may theoretically warm your
heart, it will probably wear it out, too.

Q Are electric toothbrushes better than regular toothbrushes?

A The evidence says yes, but only if you choose the right type.
In April 2005, an independent health care watchdog group,
the Cochrane Collaboration, published an analysis of data from
forty-two separate brushing studies that had more than thirty-eight
hundred participants. Based on the research, the group concluded
that electric toothbrushes with circular brushes that rotate in
opposite directions are more effective than manual toothbrushes
and other electric models. (You can die in peace now, having
finally learned the answer to this haunting question.)

So what kind of electric toothbrush should you buy in order to
keep your chompers sparkling? According to the analysis, the
aforementioned type with rotating bristles reduced an average
of 11 percent more plaque than a regular toothbrush over the

course of one to three months. After more than three months of use, rotating-head brushes reduced the signs of gingivitis (gum inflammation) by an average of 17 percent. The analysis didn't find conclusive evidence that other electric models, like the ones with brushes that move from side to side or ionic brushes, are more effective than manual brushes.

But the cheap bastards among us can take heart: Some experts maintain that a good old manual toothbrush is all you really need. In reaction to the Cochrane Collaboration study, the director of the American Dental Association's Seal of Acceptance program, Dr. Cliff Whall, downplayed the benefits of an electric toothbrush. According to Whall, as long as you brush correctly twice a day, floss once a day, and visit a dentist regularly, you're not doing yourself any harm by sticking to the manual method. Now that we've cleared this one up, you can start pondering other all-important topics, like why scratching relieves itching or whether you should wait an hour after eating before you jump into the swimming pool.

Q Does drinking too much booze kill brain cells?

A After a few innings of listening to that drunken idiot sitting behind you at the ballgame, you may begin to wonder if he had any brain cells to begin with. There's no way a few pints of alcohol could render somebody that stupid that fast, right?

The belief that alcohol kills brain cells is so pervasive that we've all come to accept it either as a fact or, at the very least, an adequate cautionary tale. But it's an idea that was perpetuated during the temperance movement, along with the claim that people who have alcohol in their blood risk bursting into flames and being burned alive. (If this were true, think of what one well-placed match could do to improve your experience at the ballgame.)

Scientific research on the brains of alcoholics has determined fairly conclusively that drinking alcohol—even a lot of it—will not kill any of your brain cells. In fact, it's been observed that moderate alcohol consumption can actually improve cognitive skills and memory.

But before you run out and start pounding down cold ones in an attempt to become a genius, remember that the emphasis should be on the word "moderate." While alcohol consumption won't kill your brain cells, excessive drinking can temporarily inhibit the creation of new brain cells. At least that was the case with laboratory rats that were subjected to binges of alcohol. Once they stopped hitting the sauce, however, the rats were again able to renew their gray matter.

Even if alcohol abuse doesn't actually kill your brain, it can definitely damage it. Studies have shown that alcohol harms the dendrites of the brain cells in your cerebellum, the learning and physical coordination center of your brain. Dendrites are the parts of the cell that receive the electrical signals from the surrounding cells; when their function is impaired, it can hurt your ability to think. As you can see, you don't want to mess with your dendrites.

So even though excessive drinking won't destroy your brain cells, you should probably try to take care of them anyway—especially since we can't vouch for how many you had in the first place.

Q Is it possible for an ape and a human to produce offspring?

A horse getting it on with a donkey can lead to a mule, an amorous encounter between a tigress and a lion can produce liger cubs, and hot donkey-on-zebra action can result in a bouncing baby zonkey. So why couldn't there be a humanzee or chuman? There's no evidence that such a creature has ever existed, but scientists haven't ruled out the possibility that one could be born.

Over time, the DNA in two species with a common ancestor will mutate to the point that the animals can no longer interbreed. It's not clear where this line is, however. Genetic analysis suggests that chimpanzees and humans split from a common ancestor about 6.3 million years ago and that they may have continued to intermittently interbreed for another nine hundred thousand years or so. Although chimpanzees and humans may seem far removed from a common ancestor, consider that 98 percent of their DNA is the same. The possibility, then, of mating a chimp and a human isn't as far-fetched as you might think.

Has anyone ever tried to do it? Yes, at least one person. In the mid-1920s curiosity got the better of a Russian scientist named Ilya Ivanovich Ivanov, and he set out to make a chimpanzee-human love child in a Guinea lab. After three unsuccessful attempts at artificially inseminating a female chimp with human sperm, Ivanov turned his attention to artificially inseminating a woman with chimpanzee sperm. He contacted a hospital in the Congo about the possibility of inseminating human patients without their knowledge. Even though he left out the "chimp" part, the hospital declined his offer.

A frustrated Ivanov went back to Russia with a male orangutan in tow, hoping to take care of business on his home turf. Remarkably, he found a few female volunteers, but they never got the chance to give it a go: The orangutan died before Ivanov could enact his devious reproductive plan. It wasn't long before Ivanov wound up in prison, and he apparently never got back into the mad scientist game.

Humanzee fever didn't fade away, though. In the 1970s, a lot of people started wondering about the origins of a peculiar chimp named Oliver. He walks on two legs; has a bald, somewhat human-like head; smells better than most chimps; and has reportedly made passes at ladies (the human kind). But genetic testing in 1996 proved that while Oliver is abnormal, he's 100 percent chimpanzee.

Today scientists are producing human-animal hybrids by injecting human stem cells into animal embryos. This has led to mouse fetuses that have small percentages of human brain cells, sheep that have partially human livers, and pigs that have human blood. The technology exists, then, to create a human-chimpanzee hybrid. But no one has dared to cross that controversial line. Yet.

Q Why doesn't liquor freeze?

A Remember the bottle of Jägermeister that was in your dad's freezer for close to fifteen years, always sloshing around, seemingly impervious to both temperature and time? Why didn't that bottle of booze ever freeze?

Actually, liquor does freeze, just at an extremely frigid temperature. According to research conducted at Purdue University, the freezing point of ethyl alcohol (the type found in alcoholic beverages) is −179.1 degrees Fahrenheit. Household freezers don't get anywhere near that cold, so they're not going to turn your liquor into a block of ice.

But what about the emergency six-pack of Budweiser that you keep stashed in your garage? Why does the beer turn to slush when the temperature drops into the twenties? Simple: A twelve-ounce can of Budweiser contains about 5 percent alcohol by volume. The other 95 percent or so of that tasty beverage is made up of water, as well as some hops, malts, and other flavorings. Water, of course, freezes at thirty-two degrees Fahrenheit. Because your Budweiser contains such a small amount of alcohol and such a large amount of easily freezable water, it will seem like the whole thing is frozen. As for the ancient bottle of Jägermeister in Dad's freezer? It contained enough alcohol—35 percent—to avert such blatant slushiness issues.

Think about that the next time you trot out to your garage on a winter evening and crack open a cold one.

Q How do bugs know you're about to squish them?

A With some natural aptitude and years of training in an Eastern monastery, you may acquire certain fighting skills that let you drop a grown man to his knees in an instant—but even the most agile martial arts master struggles when it's time to swat a fly. Why? Insects may be tiny and powerless, but they have adaptations that give them an edge against the many larger forms of life that want to do them in.

For starters, the bugs that you most want to squish—flies, cockroaches, and the like—are equipped with compound eyes. A compound eye is a collection of structures called ommatidia. A fly, for example, has four thousand ommatidia in each eye; each ommatidium has its own light-sensing cells and a focusing lens that's positioned for a unique field of view. Collectively, the elements of a compound eye produce a panoramic vision of the bug's surroundings. The resolution of the resulting image isn't so hot, but it does the trick for detecting sudden movements from almost any direction.

Even when their supercharged vision fails them, insects have other ways to escape your wrath. Many bugs can actually feel the flyswatter approaching thanks to special sensory hairs called setae. When you start your bug-smashing motion, you push air between you and your target. This shift in air pressure stimulates the bug's setae, which signal the brain that something is coming. The movement of the setae gives the bug an idea of where the threat is coming from, and the bug reacts by scurrying in the opposite direction.

It also helps that some bugs are thinking about their getaways before it even seems necessary. In 2008, biologists at the California Institute of Technology used high-speed cameras to observe a group of flies. They found that it takes less than a tenth of a second for a fly to identify a potential threat, plan an escape route, and position its legs for optimal take-off. In other words, when you're sneaking up on a fly and getting ready to strike, that fly has probably already spotted you and is prepared to zip away. This little bit of extra preparation helps pave the way for a Houdini-like escape.

Will the valuable information gleaned from this research enable us to finally gain the upper hand—quite literally—in our ongoing chess match against bugs? Don't count on it.

Q How did people wake up before there were alarm clocks?

A Everyone has a trick for waking up on time. Some people put the alarm clock across the room so that they have to get out of bed to turn it off; some set the clock ahead by ten or fifteen minutes to try to fool themselves into thinking that it's later than it is; some set multiple alarms; and some—those boring Goody Two-Shoes types—simply go to bed at a reasonable hour and get enough sleep.

We don't necessarily rely on it every day, and some of us definitely don't obey it very often, but just about everybody has an alarm clock. How did people ever wake up before these modern marvels existed?

Many of the tough problems in life have a common solution: hire someone else to do it. Long ago in England, you could hire a guy to come by each morning and, using a long pole, knock on your bedroom window to wake you up so that you would get to work on time. This practice began during the Industrial Revolution of the late eighteenth century, when getting to work on time was a new and innovative idea. (In the grand tradition of British terminology that makes Americans snicker, the pole operator was known as a "knocker-up.") There's no word on how said pole operator managed to get himself up on time, but we can guess.

The truth is, you don't need any type of alarm, and you never did. Or so science tells us. Your body's circadian rhythms give you a sort of natural wake-up call via your body temperature's daily fluctuation. It rises every morning regardless of when you went to bed. Studies conducted at Harvard University seem to indicate that this rising temperature wakes us up (if the alarm hasn't already gone off).

Another study, conducted at the University of Lubeck in Germany, found that people have an innate ability to wake themselves up very early if they anticipate it beforehand. One night, the researchers told fifteen subjects that they would be awakened at 6:00 AM. Around 4:30 AM, the researchers noticed that the subjects began to experience a rise in the stress hormone adrenocorticotropin. On the other two nights, the subjects were told that they would get a 9:00 AM wake-up call—but those diligent scientists shook them out of bed three hours early, at 6:00 AM. And this time, the adrenocorticotropin levels of the subjects held steady in the early morning hours.

It seems, then, that humans relied on their bodies to rouse them from the dream world long before a knocker-up or an alarm clock ever existed.

Q What do weasels have to do with coffee?

A So you've heard the stories and you swear that you'd never drink coffee made from beans that have passed through a weasel's digestive tract. Luckily, you'll never get the opportunity. Those ultra-gourmet beans that sell for anywhere from one to six hundred dollars a pound didn't come out of a weasel. The animal in question is actually the Asian palm civet. Does that make you feel better?

No? Perhaps you're like columnist Dave Barry, who dismisses the stuff as "poopacino" and thinks the whole craze for exotic brews is nothing but a tempest in a coffee cup. But kopi luwak, as it is known in Indonesia, got a big thumbs-up from Oprah Winfrey in 2003 when representatives of the Coffee Critic, a Ukiah, California, coffee shop, offered her a taste. Winfrey gamely took a sip right on her show and declared the so-called "weasel coffee" eminently fit to drink. (Barry, for the record, opines that it "tastes like somebody washed a dead cat in it." Take your pick.)

What's the story here? The Asian palm civet, or luwak, is a small nocturnal mammal that's native to Indonesia, southern India, East Africa, Southeast Asia, the Philippines, and the south coast of China. By all accounts, luwaks are particularly fond of ripe coffee fruit. They digest the flesh of the fruit and excrete the beans, which are then gathered by grateful coffee farmers. So what's the attraction? According to one theory, the acids in the luwak's stomach dissolve the proteins in the coatings of the beans that cause the bitter aftertaste that accompanies more traditional blends. When brewed, kopi luwak supposedly has a mellower and sweeter flavor than regular java.

This theory has been put to the test by researchers at Canada's University of Guelph. In 2004, food science professor Massimo Marcone concluded that lactic acid bacteria in the luwak's digestive tract do indeed leach some of the proteins from the beans' outer shells. (It should be noted that most people in blind taste tests conducted by the same researchers could not tell the difference between kopi luwak and other coffees.) Marcone, who collected his own beans in Ethiopia and Indonesia, allayed fears of contamination by pointing out that coffee producers in Asia wash the luwak-derived beans extensively in order to banish any lingering bacteria.

No one knows who first decided to clean and roast the luwak's droppings. Kopi luwak was cherished in Asia long before Western importers decided to capitalize on its rarity and unusual origins. And capitalize they do: A single cup in one of the few American bistros that serves it will cost significantly more than normal joe. Who would have thought that a pile of poop could be transformed into a pot of gold?

Chapter Three

HEALTH MATTERS

Q Can people get fat because of a slow metabolism?

A Your metabolism gets way more blame than it should for that spare tire you call a stomach. The fact is, a slow metabolism is rarely the primary reason for excessive weight gain.

Broadly speaking, your metabolism comprises all the chemical processes your cells undertake to sustain life. But when people talk about a fast or slow metabolism, they generally mean the basal metabolic rate—the rate at which the body turns nutrients into energy (burning calories) when at rest. While it's true that genetics plays a role in defining the baseline for this rate and that some people naturally burn more calories than others, very few folks have metabolic rates that are slow enough to single-handedly make them fat. The main culprit is almost always too many calories or too little exercise (or both).

The body's metabolic rate is highly flexible—it changes with your habits. For example, you can speed it up somewhat by adding more muscle; muscle burns more calories while you're at rest than fat does. On the other hand, you can slow your metabolism down through inactivity. And if your metabolism is naturally slow and you don't work out enough, you'll probably put on weight faster than somebody who has a quicker metabolism and doesn't exercise much. So if you haven't already gotten the hint, read the following words very, very carefully: Get off your keister and join a health club.

Oh, and one more thing: In a cruel twist of fate, serious dieting tends to slow down the metabolism. If you cut back drastically on your caloric intake, the body typically enters "starvation mode"— it reacts to a perceived lack of available food by storing fat. Ain't biology a bitch?

Q Are procrastinators lazy?

A We'll apply all of our brainpower to this question, but first we have to clean up our desks and pay a few bills, okay? Just kidding (sort of).

The easiest way to explain why some people procrastinate is to say that they're lazy. After all, if something needs to be done and someone's not doing it, doesn't that seem irresponsible? And isn't laziness irresponsible?

But the fact is, procrastinators are almost anything but lazy. Why, then, do people procrastinate? There are a number of reasons, starting with disorganization. Some disorganized folks can be termed "lumpers"—people who lump every task into one hard-to-finish whole and become frustrated when stuff doesn't get done. They simply aren't adept at subdividing all of their tasks into an achievable plan. Therefore, they don't accomplish things in a timely manner and are thought to be lazy.

Distractibility is another culprit. The procrastinators who fall into this category may have problems that are physical at their roots, such as attention deficit disorder. If you're unable to focus on the task at hand, completing it is going to be awfully tough.

Some people are perfectionists; they're unable to finish something unless they feel as though it's just right. And others are simply afraid of failing; put the task off long enough, and eventually you might not have to do it. Either way, certain powerful emotions prevent procrastinators from getting the job done, which is a far cry from laziness.

Okay, we've had enough. Once we watch today's *The King of Queens* rerun, we'll continue working on this book.

Q How much booze can you drink without dying?

A A long-suffering fan of the Chicago Cubs must have thought up this question.

Unfortunately, Cubs fans won't find any easy answers here about how much booze they can safely pound during the next soul-crushing defeat. That's because the amount of alcohol that somebody can ingest without dying depends on a huge number of factors. Nevertheless, we can provide some rough guidelines for understanding how alcohol works on the body.

Since we're talking about Cubs fans, let's speak in terms of beer. (For those with broader tastes, experts identify one drink as a twelve-ounce beer, a 1.5-ounce shot, or a five-ounce glass of wine, each of which contains about the same amount of alcohol.) Once imbibed, alcohol enters the bloodstream through the lining of the stomach and small intestine. Most of it is processed and eliminated by the liver (cirrhosis, anyone?)—but the liver can only work so quickly, usually taking care of a little less than one drink's worth per hour. Excess alcohol waits in the bloodstream until the liver can eliminate it.

Drunkenness is gauged by blood alcohol concentration (BAC). BAC measures the percentage of alcohol in the bloodstream at any given time; because heavier people usually have more blood, BAC can be interpreted as a ratio of alcohol-to-body weight. That's why men, who are usually heavier than women, can often drink more than females without appearing drunk. But BAC varies based on many other factors, like the presence of medications in the bloodstream.

Below, we outline the effects of different BAC levels. (A BAC of .01 is one part alcohol to ten thousand parts blood, a BAC of .02 is two parts alcohol to ten thousand parts blood, a BAC of .03 is three parts alcohol to ten thousand parts blood, and so on.)

- .02–.03. A slight elevation of mood; few noticeable effects. As this is generally well before the first pitch, Cubs fans may still be optimistic about the day's game.

- .05–.06. Feelings of relaxation and mild sedation; slightly impaired judgment. This is still well before game time for most Wrigley Field bleacher bums.

- .07–.09. Impaired motor coordination; impaired speech. Cubs fans may have feelings of elation/depression while singing the national anthem.

- .11–.12. Impaired coordination and balance; poor judgment. This is when Cubs fans may accidentally spill their beers into the outfield basket while reaching for a home run that's just been hit by the opposing team.

- .14–.15. Serious problems with motor coordination and judgment; slurred speech; blurred vision. This may be around the third inning, when it seems wise to run onto the field.

- .20. Mental confusion; loss of motor control. Around now, a Cubs fan may start arguing vehemently with the guy next to him that Thad Bosley should be in the Hall of Fame.

- .30. Severe intoxication; hospitalization is necessary. Forget the game—death could result.

- .40–.60. Unconsciousness; coma; possible death. This is not good.

As we said, the number of drinks it would require to reach these levels of BAC varies. But for the typical two-hundred-pound man (this may seem a little heavy, but hey, we're talking about Chicagoans here), one drink in an hour raises his BAC to .02; if the same man were to drink ten Old Styles in that same hour, it would skyrocket to about .19. In order to reach .35 (a level at which some deaths have been reported), he'd have to drink nineteen or twenty Old Styles in an hour.

Because the liver can only work so fast—it can lower the BAC by about .015 per hour, regardless of gender and body weight—the BAC won't decrease at the same rate as it went up. So considering that alcohol sales at Wrigley Field halt after the seventh inning— about two hours into the game—our two-hundred-pound Cubs fan would be able to slam about twenty or twenty-one ridiculously overpriced beers without reaching a lethal BAC level. Then again, our theoretical Cubs fan already knew that.

Q Is it bad to exercise when you're sick?

A As excuses for blowing off the gym go, being under the weather is reasonably legit.

Doctors refer to the "rule of neck" for gauging when it's all right to exercise. If you have symptoms below the neck—such as a hacking cough, congestion in the chest, muscle aches, or an upset stomach—it's best to skip your workout. These symptoms indicate something more serious than the ordinary sniffles, like the flu or bronchitis. Depleting your energy reserves and putting stress on your lungs can make you feel worse and impair your immune system's ability to fight off the ailment. And if you have a fever, exercise is an especially bad idea—exerting yourself can lead to inflammation of the heart and major dehydration.

However, if you have symptoms that are isolated above the neck—general stuffiness and a slight sore throat—you're probably just suffering from a mild cold. In this case, light exercise should be okay.

But even then, you don't want to overdo it. Wearing yourself out does just that—it expends the energy that you need to blast the bug out of your system. And no, it doesn't help to "sweat out" the toxins. It's also not especially considerate to pass on your germs to everyone else at the gym.

The best advice? Play it safe. If you're under the weather, you officially have our permission to be a lazy S.O.B. Feel free to spend some quality time with your beloved couch and watch a bunch of *Seinfeld* reruns.

Q Why doesn't your stomach digest itself?

A Your stomach is the fourth stop on the amazing journey along the digestive tract (after the mouth, pharynx, and esophagus), but it's the point where the system gets down to serious business.

Cells in the stomach produce two to three quarts of hydrochloric acid and digestive enzymes daily, and muscles work to churn everything together in order to create a soupy goo. This digestive gastric juice is potent stuff—it's strong enough to break down wood and metal, let alone food. And the only thing that keeps it from eating through your body is a thin layer of equally powerful mucus.

Acids are dangerous because when they are dissolved in water, they release excess hydrogen ions (hydrogen atoms with a positive charge). These ions react easily and quickly with other material, breaking chemical compounds down into simpler compounds. In the stomach, the hydrogen ions combine with protein compounds in food to form amino acids and simpler polypeptide compounds that the small and large intestines can further digest.

The stomach wall is made up of vulnerable proteins, which means that you would be in big trouble if hydrochloric acid were to reach it. Luckily, the stomach surface is lined with cells that continually secrete mucus that neutralizes the acid; this mucus is loaded with bicarbonate, a powerful chemical base. (A base is essentially the opposite of an acid.)

When bicarbonate is dissolved into water, it results in the release of hydroxide ions, which have a negative charge. Negative hydroxide ions and positive hydrogen ions effectively cancel each other out if they are combined; the chemicals undergo a reaction and form water and other harmless products.

The system works well, but since it depends on constant chemical balance, it isn't entirely foolproof. Sometimes acid will erode part of this mucus, resulting in a painful gastric ulcer in the stomach lining. In extreme cases, the acid will erode a hole all the way through the stomach wall, and the stomach's contents will spill out into the abdominal cavity.

Fortunately, the stomach lining keeps most of us safe, even when we eat like pigs. So next Thanksgiving, remember to count mucus among your blessings.

Q Do people really die from laughing?

A Surely you're familiar with this phrase: "I nearly died laughing." You've probably used it multiple times just while reading this book—you may have even said it right now. Gosh, when you think about it, it's really sort of a miracle that you've made it this far. That's because dying from laughter isn't just a figure of speech—people really have keeled over due to cases of the giggles.

The phrase "dying from laughter," or "die laughing," dates back to the sixteenth century, and its endurance in the language may have to do with the disturbing number of deaths, both recorded and anecdotal, that have been connected to laughing fits. One of the first to succumb to giddiness was the Stoic Greek philosopher Chrysippus in 207 or 206 BC.

The story goes something like this: Chrysippus fed his donkey some wine. (We're not sure why he would do this, but Greek philosophers were known to have some unusual tastes.) A drunk donkey is funny enough, but here's the "killer": The donkey then tried to eat some figs! Evidently, the sight of a donkey eating figs was just too much for a Stoic to bear, and Chrysippus keeled over mid-chortle.

Over the ensuing two thousand years, a number of other deaths reportedly have been caused by laughter. The casualties have included a British bricklayer who was watching a sitcom called *The Goodies* (it is unclear whether this man died from laughter or stupidity) and a Danish physician who was watching one of John Cleese's scenes in *A Fish Called Wanda*.

It isn't entirely clear if laughter actually caused these deaths or if it merely acted as a catalyst for other conditions. For example, studies have shown that cataplexy (a condition in narcoleptics that causes seizures) can be triggered by strong emotional responses such as laughter, while other research has suggested that laughter may cause heart attacks in people who are already susceptible to them.

However, there is one documented disease in which laughter is a primary symptom. Kuru—a.k.a. "the laughing disease"—plagued the indigenous people of New Guinea during the turn of the twentieth century. This degenerative viral disease is largely spread through ritual cannibalism, however, so most of us don't need to worry about contracting it.

Many health experts believe that laughter is more apt to help than harm you. Some research indicates that laughter may play a role in increasing amounts of the antibody immunoglobin A, which fights bacterial and viral infections. So there's no need to worry— reading this hilarious book isn't going to kill you. It might even make you healthier.

Q Are tanning beds safer than sun exposure?

A Tanning beds may protect naturally pale people from snickers at the beach, but there's no evidence that they guard against the health risks associated with old-fashioned sun worship.

Tanning is a defensive reaction to ultraviolet (UV) radiation, which means it's an indication of skin damage. When the skin sustains damage from UV rays, it produces the brown pigment melanin to help protect against future radiation. Cancer researchers believe that exposure to UV radiation significantly increases the risk of both melanoma and non-melanoma skin cancers. Your body might not effectively repair the resulting damage to its DNA, which can lead to mutations that cause cancer.

So unless your tan comes from a spray bottle, you're increasing your cancer risk. Tanning salons sometimes claim that tanning beds are safer than the sun because they use "moderate" amounts of UVA radiation and even less UVB radiation, which was once thought to be the more dangerous of the two. But research doesn't support this assertion.

In a study published in 2001, researchers at Johns Hopkins School of Medicine and the University of Manchester in England exposed eleven people to ten tanning bed sessions apiece over two weeks. After the sessions were completed, the researchers examined skin and blood samples for signs of molecular change. One such marker is the presence of cyclobutane pyrimidine dimer, which indicates that there has been DNA damage from UV radiation; another is the presence of the p53 protein, which shows that the body is working to repair itself. Both signify the sort of UV damage to cells that can eventually cause cancer, and both were found in all of the participants. The researchers concluded that the damage from a tanning bed session is on par with a day at the beach.

It doesn't appear as if there's such a thing as a safe tan. For the pale-skinned, the choices are to risk cancer, risk turning orange with a spray-on tan, or suck it up and strut onto the beach flaunting pasty flesh that's slathered in sunscreen.

Q Do cigarettes stunt your growth?

A Remember all of those questionable warnings that your mother gave you when you were a kid? Like the one about how if you made a funny face, it might get stuck that way? Or the various ways that you might go blind—such as reading in dim light, sitting too close to the television, or getting a little too, um, friendly with yourself? They seem pretty humorous now.

But Mom may have been on to something when she told you that smoking would stunt your growth. Some of Mom's friends at the University of Montreal conducted a study, published in 2008, of nearly thirteen hundred teenage smokers and compared them to non-smoking teens. They found that boys who smoked were on average about 2.5 centimeters shorter than boys who didn't smoke.

The girls who smoked weren't any shorter than their non-smoking counterparts, but they also weren't any thinner, apparently dispelling the commonly held belief that smoking can help you control your weight. Height and body mass indexes among smoking girls were the same as among non-smoking girls.

You now know that your mother's pearls of wisdom could sometimes stretch the truth; after all, you can still read this page just fine after years and years of ... let's just say, sitting too close to the TV. But when it comes to smoking, it turns out that Mom wasn't just spouting an old wives' tale.

Q Are you more likely to break a bone putting on your underwear or jumping on a trampoline?

A Is putting on your underwear more dangerous than doing that double layout somersault on the trampoline? It depends on how old you are. According to a study by doctors at Rhode Island Children's Hospital and Brown University, trampoline injuries sent more than half a million children to emergency rooms between 2000 and 2005. About 168,400 of those injuries were classified as fractures and dislocations, and the vast majority of patients were between five and twelve years old.

Those who are not professional acrobats tend to leave trampolines behind as they get older. Few people, however, abandon wearing underwear. How do most people put on their underwear? One foot at a time, which can leave you balanced precariously on one leg while trying to insert the other into the open leg hole.

Humans tend to lose their ability to maintain balance as they get older. Each year, more than three hundred thousand Americans ages sixty-five and older suffer hip fractures that are related to falls. A survey by Yale University revealed that most of these falls occur in the home, with living rooms, bedrooms, and hallways being the riskiest locations. Most people put their underwear on in the bedroom, so it's plausible that some hip fractures can be the result of the falling-while-putting-on-underwear syndrome.

Saga, a British insurance company, reported that 371 people in the United Kingdom were hospitalized in 1998 due to injuries that they incurred while putting on their underwear. Saga's statistics, though, didn't indicate the ages of the individuals or the extent of their injuries. That's a relatively small segment of the population, but it might simply reflect the number of people who weren't embarrassed to confess that they had an accident while slipping into their skivvies.

What's the best way to reduce falls, including those that are underwear-related? The *Merck Manual of Aging* suggests keeping a slip-proof mat in the bedroom and clearing the floor of dangerous clutter. And there is a foolproof method for putting on your underwear safely: Sit down, insert both feet into the leg holes, plant your feet firmly on the floor, and grab the waistband and pull it while standing up. If done correctly, this will result in your underwear being secured to your body without injury. Children use this nifty method when they are learning how to dress themselves. Grandparents might find it quite effective, too.

What about trampolines? If you are an average recreational user, the U.S. Consumer Products Safety Commission recommends that you avoid fancy tricks if you want to land on your feet. Review the tips on the commission's Web site and bouncing on a trampoline will be as safe as, well, putting on your underwear.

Q Can somebody be more than three sheets to the wind?

A Drunk as a lord. Hammered. Trashed. Smashed. Blasted. Blotto. The English language has hundreds of euphemisms for drunkenness, but there's one we've never really understood: three sheets to the wind. Why not a baker's dozen? What does a sheet in the wind have to do with being drunk?

Like many other phrases that don't seem to make a lot of sense, this one has its origin in seafaring jargon. In this case, a "sheet" is not what most of us would expect (say, a sheet of paper or a sheet on a bed). It's a term for a rope—specifically, the rope that secures the sail to the body of the boat.

Aside from their obvious use as a handy means for swinging during swashbuckling sword fights, these sheets play a critical role in controlling the sail. When one of them comes loose, the ship veers and wobbles like a drunk fiddler. If two of them detach, the ship is really in trouble. And a ship with three sheets flung to the wind will lurch uncontrollably.

Is it possible to be more than three sheets to the wind? Technically, yes—it all depends on how many sheets a ship has. A double topsail schooner, for example, has at least four sheets. In fact, there was a time when you could be "four sheets to the wind." When the sheet metaphor was first coined, sailors had a shorthand way to rate the relative drunkenness of their cohorts, from one sheet (light-headed) to four sheets (unconscious).

Today, there's a more accurate way to gauge drunkenness: It's called a breathalyzer.

Q How many rare diseases are there?

A Most of us are lucky: We weren't born with Hutchinson-Gilford progeria syndrome (HGPS), a disease with symptoms that are similar to premature aging and leaves, say, a twelve-year-old struggling with the hardened arteries of a seventy-year-old. HGPS is one of the rarest diseases in the world—as of 2008, only forty-some children were known to have it.

What makes a disease rare? In the United States, the National Institutes of Health generally consider a rare disease to be one that affects fewer than two hundred thousand people in the nation. The European Organization for Rare Diseases (EURODIS) defines a rare disease as one that affects fewer than one out of every two thousand individuals in the European Union. In Japan, a disease that affects fewer than fifty thousand people out of the total population is considered rare.

EURODIS states that there are currently between six thousand and eight thousand rare diseases afflicting the human race. What do we know about them? According to some estimates, genetic mutations cause about 80 percent of all rare diseases; most of the remaining 20 percent stem from bacterial or viral infections, allergic reactions, or environmental toxins. But the causes of most rare diseases are poorly understood.

You may have noticed that a lot of stories in the media about rare diseases involve children. It's not just because kids have a lot of heart-tugging appeal. Many rare diseases lead to early mortality, so kids are likely to be the only people who have them. Nearly 75 percent of all those suffering from rare diseases are children; 30 percent of those victims will not live beyond the age of five. Approximately 3 to 4 percent of all children are born with a rare disease, and the number may even be a little higher because many kids receive the wrong diagnosis or, in poor and underdeveloped areas, no diagnosis at all.

What can we do about rare diseases? In 1983, the U.S. Congress passed the Orphan Drug Act, which provides financial incentives for pharmaceutical companies to develop drug-based therapies. As of 2008, the Food and Drug Administration's Office of Orphan Product Development had certified 269 drugs for the market and had given financial incentives for research on more than 1,449 experimental drugs that were in the pipeline. European governments have passed similar legislation to aid researchers.

To raise public awareness, EURODIS, the American National Organization of Rare Disorders, and other similar organizations around the world have designated the last day of February as Rare Disease Day. Every four years, it falls on the "rare" date of February 29, giving leap year special meaning for those who are awaiting something that's even rarer than their disease: a cure.

Q Who took care of the aged and poor before Social Security and welfare programs?

A Just about everyone—except the government. For centuries, up to the Great Depression of the 1930s, families traditionally took care of grandparents and aging parents. Imagine Nana and Poppa sharing your kitchen, your outhouse, your fireplace, and maybe even your bedroom. Now you know why people in those nineteenth-century daguerreotypes never smiled.

Few people had health insurance, so if someone lost a job or broke a leg, family members were expected to provide support. If that wasn't enough to keep bread on the table, churches, fraternal clubs, and lodges had special funds to aid families in need. The Red Cross and other organizations like it also stood ready to help. In big cities, where immigrant populations were high, aid societies for different ethnic groups sprang up to offer loans, employment, and even shelter during tough periods.

The system worked fairly well for a long time. But when the stock market crashed in 1929 and the Great Depression ensued, charitable organizations were overwhelmed. Basically, they had functioned by soliciting donations from the wealthy, but now many of these well-to-do citizens were impoverished, too. The crash and subsequent bank failures wiped out the savings of countless families, wages plummeted, businesses closed at a frightening rate, and nationwide unemployment averaged 25 percent.

President Herbert Hoover refused to put more money into employment programs or relief—he was not about to turn the government into a welfare agency. But the Depression deepened, and by the end of his term, the embattled Hoover, a Republican, approved giving states big federal loans that were to be distributed to the needy. But it was too little, too late. Hoover was voted out of office—he was replaced by a Democrat, Franklin Delano Roosevelt.

In the mid-1930s, Roosevelt's New Deal programs set up Social Security as old-age and disability insurance, not as a charity. Roosevelt also designated millions of federal dollars to programs that put people back to work, and he convinced states to start unemployment insurance. The U.S. government has been in the welfare business ever since.

Q Why hasn't anyone found a cure for the common cold?

A For one thing, there's no such disease. The so-called common cold is actually a set of general symptoms that are associated with more than two hundred separate virus strains. The worst offenders are varieties of rhinovirus, which causes 10 to 40 percent of colds, but coronaviruses and other virus families produce their fair shares of colds as well.

When a virus infects your upper-respiratory system—by invading your body's cells and using the cells' energy to replicate itself—your immune system sends in white blood cells to fight it. If you've never been infected by that particular virus strain, the immune system doesn't know how to destroy the virus, so the initial attack against it isn't successful. The battle rages on until your immune system figures out how to knock out the virus. The results of the fight are tissue inflammation and a lot of mucus, which cause congestion, a sore throat, coughing, a runny nose, and sneezing. All this hacking and dripping expel the virus from your body.

So finding a cure for the common cold actually means dealing with hundreds of separate viruses, some of which scientists haven't even identified yet. The good news is that once you've been infected by a virus, your immune system can usually recognize that particular strain when it shows up again and knock it out immediately. The bad news is that cold viruses keep pace with the immune system by mutating. As the virus strains change, the body doesn't recognize them anymore—it's a never-ending arms race.

Furthermore, finding a cure for the common cold isn't exactly the top priority within the medical community—researchers have bigger fish to fry, such as cancer, diabetes, heart disease, and a long list of other afflictions. Besides, people typically bounce back from a cold within a week or so.

There are, however, scientists who are working on a cure for the common cold, and they've made some progress. In February 2009, researchers from the University of Maryland and the University of Wisconsin announced that they had decoded the genome for ninety-nine strains of rhinovirus, which, as we said, is the main cold virus. They mapped the relationships among the strains as if they were assembling a family tree. This information revealed some persistent commonalities among the strains, which could pave the way for future treatments.

In the meantime, the best cure for the common cold is your immune system's attack on the virus. Or put another way, the best cure for the common cold is the common cold.

Q Why are we afraid of bugs?

A The biggest reason is a good one: They can kill us. Now, onto the more subtle stuff. One function of bugs from an ecological point of view is to spread small particles, such as pollen or the nutrients in their digestive leavings. Bugs also help dead plants and animals to decompose, enriching the soil in the process. And some larger animals, like birds and lizards, like to feast on bugs, so insects are an important link in the food chain. These critters may be little, but without them, the world as we know it wouldn't exist.

So why are we so afraid of them? There are a number of theories, including good old human evolution. Our innate fear of bugs may be triggered by genes that were advantageous to our ancestors. This fear helped them to dodge the deadly superbugs of the distant past, allowing them to thrive and pass their bug-hating genes on through the generations.

However, it's possible that the fear of bugs isn't innate at all—some scientists look at it as a cultural rather than a biological phenomenon, a product of our contemporary way of life. We want our homes to be sterile and free from any dirt; we practice far more elaborate hygiene than our ancestors did, constantly scrubbing ourselves with antibacterial soaps; and we live in cities and suburbs where nature is tightly controlled, where chemically treated lawns are free from undesirable pests and grasses. In this sanitized environment, bugs can seem almost like overgrown microbes or germs, soiling our spotless floors and crawling into our clean bedrooms and closets. Bugs symbolize disease and disorder.

Or maybe bugs disgust us because their societies undermine some of our most cherished beliefs. It's deeply ingrained in us to value our individuality, and one psychologist has suggested that we hate bugs in part because their existence calls this individuality into question. The sight of hundreds or even thousands of insects swarming or toiling mindlessly in the hive threatens our own sense of uniqueness and independence—and we loathe them for it.

But these forms of bug fear are tame compared to the psychological disorders that some unfortunate people experience. Entomophobia, for example, is a condition that is marked by a persistent, irrational fear of bug infestation. And people who have delusions of parasitosis actually believe that their bodies are teeming with bugs.

Sounds exhausting, doesn't it? Bugs do serious things to us—physically and psychologically—but as alien as they seem, they're part of our cultural lives, whether we're enjoying honey in our tea, wearing a beetle-emblem broach, or shrieking at the killer spider in a midnight movie. Next time you jump at the sight of a gross ant on your kitchen floor in mid-summer, remember that our world wouldn't exist without him and his ilk—and that he has much more reason to be afraid of you than you have to be afraid of him.

Q Can a person be intelligent but not smart?

A Very bright people are capable of doing some very dimwitted things. Take Eliot Spitzer. The former governor and attorney general of New York may have had an up-and-coming political career and a degree from Harvard, but that didn't stop him from getting caught in the middle of a high-priced prostitution ring.

And what about the heads of the "Big Three" North American automakers? In the midst of 2008's economic crisis, they traveled to Washington, D.C., to beg for twenty-five billion dollars of the taxpayers' money. The thing is, each of these guys flew to D.C. on his own private jet. Might have been a smart time to go coach.

Shouldn't these highly successful, highly intelligent people have known better? One would think so. But leading industrial psychologist Mortimer Feinberg says that the dark side of being bright is that one can actually be sabotaged by one's own intellect. In his book *Why Smart People Do Dumb Things: Lessons from the New Science of Behavioral Economics,* Feinberg explains: "Intelligent people run the risk of self-destruction caused by their own brilliance. That self-destruction is caused by a virus that flourishes within strong intellects. And there is no escape. If you possess above-average intelligence you already have the virus. It comes with the high IQ territory."

The virus is what Feinberg calls Self-Destructive Intelligence Syndrome. And people who have it often fall prey to one of what he calls the Four Pillars of Stupidity: There's hubris (pride to the point that one no longer fears public opinion); arrogance (feeling entitled to anything and everything one wants); narcissism (self-absorption to the point that one is blind to reality); and the unconscious need to fail (apparently, some highly intelligent people just can't handle the pressure of being so brainy).

Perhaps this helps to shed some light on what happened to Stephen Chao. In 1992, the Harvard MBA and media-biz whiz was climbing the ranks as the newly crowned president of Fox News. But that didn't prevent him from making a huge, lame-brained blunder. Invited to speak at a management conference for Fox executives, board members, and world dignitaries—including Fox owner Rupert Murdoch, U.S. defense secretary Dick Cheney, and National Endowment for the Humanities chairwoman Lynne Cheney—Chao decided that it would be a fabulous idea to hire a male stripper to perform in the middle of his talk. (The topic was censorship, after all.)

And so the stripper took off his clothes (right beside Lynne Cheney, as fate would have it), and Chao was immediately fired. Things went even further south for him from there—he ended up working at McDonald's for a while. But, hey, he was hardly the first person of high intelligence to crash and burn. Sometimes it takes real brains to be so brainless.

Q Why do toddlers get so many ear infections?

A To torture sleep-deprived parents? That's part of the equation, yes. Ear infections (a.k.a. *otitis media*) are as much a part of raising kids as mind-grating Barney sing-alongs and embarrassing public tantrums.

In the United States, ear infections are the second-most common illness for children, just behind colds. The two usually go together, in fact. For kids who are six months to three years of age, 61 percent of colds are accompanied by ear infections.

Typically, an ear infection occurs when fluid buildup and inflammation from a cold blocks the Eustachian tube, the passageway that runs between the back of the nose and throat to the middle ear. With this tube blocked, fluid in the middle ear can't escape and builds up behind the eardrum, creating an ideal breeding ground for bacteria and viruses. This happens more often in young children than adults because kids have narrower and more horizontally positioned Eustachian tubes than grownups do. As a result, it's much easier for these tubes to get blocked up. Antibiotics can solve the problem pretty quickly, though that's of little consolation to a parent who hasn't slept in two nights.

Susceptibility to ear infections is usually highest for children who are between six and eighteen months. As kids get older, the Eustachian tubes grow wider and tilt more vertically, so the possibility of getting an ear infection diminishes greatly. Fortunately, kids also outgrow Barney. We wish we could say the same for public tantrums.

Q Why does the doctor want you to cough during a hernia exam?

A It's always the same icky drill during a man's annual physical: A doctor awkwardly places a few fingers on the area around the groin and asks the patient to turn his head and cough. What in the name of modern medicine is going on here? (Ladies, feel free to skip to the next question.)

Broadly speaking, a hernia is an organ or other piece of soft tissue that pokes through the cavity wall enclosing it. It typically occurs when internal organs protrude into weak spots in the muscular wall of the abdomen. This can cause painful bulges in the abdominal wall and, in some cases, even tissue death. Hernias won't go away without surgery.

The coughing exam is designed to detect the most common type of hernia, the inguinal hernia. In this variety (which accounts for 75 percent of all hernias), part of the intestines, bladder, or other tissue pokes through a weak spot in the groin muscle. Coughing tenses up your abdominal muscles. If there is a hernia, this pressure will cause it to bulge farther, so it's easier for the doctor to feel. Turning your head doesn't have much of an effect on abdominal muscles; the doctor just doesn't want to be coughed on.

Inguinal hernias are mainly a guy thing (as is the coughing test). They do occasionally occur in women, but they're five times more likely for a man. While the exam ranks pretty low on the dignity scale, it's a lot more fun than an unattended hernia, which can form a bulge as big as a basketball. Most guys will happily endure a few uncomfortable moments to ensure long-term health.

Chapter Four

TRADITIONS

Q How did high school proms get started?

A The word itself seems to have come from slang-happy college students of the late eighteen hundreds and early nineteen hundreds. It was originally a shortened form of "promenade," meaning the entry and announcement of guests at a formal dance, and then became a term for college dances in general. The earliest known reference to a prom can be found in an Amherst College student's 1894 journal entry; it likely referring to a senior class dance held at nearby Smith College.

But what about *high school* dances—proms, specifically? They are more closely related to upper-class debutante balls than to college dances. The debutante ball originated in sixteenth-century England as a formal way to present a young woman who was available for marriage. The tradition spread to America in the late nineteenth century and flourished among the wealthy as a rite of passage to adulthood. In the early twentieth century, middle-class parents wanted the opportunity to give their own kids similar tastes of adulthood, so they began organizing high school dances. References to these proms started popping up in high school year-books in the 1930s, but some communities were likely holding these events earlier than that.

Early proms were far cries from the extravaganzas of today. High school kids would dress up in their Sunday best, go to the school gym, enjoy some refreshments, and cut a rug—all under the watchful eyes of adults. Limousines and tuxedos weren't yet part of the equation.

But as America's middle class grew more prosperous in the 1950s, kids and parents spent more money on proms. In turn, the importance of these dances increased. Some schools moved them out of their gyms and into hotel ballrooms; young men started cramming themselves into formal wear, and young ladies began dropping loads of cash on special prom dresses. The popularity of proms waned a bit in the 1960s, when everybody who was anybody rebelled against everything. But proms came back strong in the mid-1980s, fueled by a popular string of romantic teen comedies, such as *Footloose* and *Pretty in Pink.*

These days, proms are big business. Some estimates place total annual U.S. prom expenditures at more than two billion dollars. In 2007, *Seventeen* magazine estimated that the girl alone drops an average of eight hundred dollars on her senior prom. That's a lot of money to spend for a date with a guy you'll probably never see again after graduation.

Q Why do men like hardware stores?

A It's common knowledge that a man will not ask for help. He'll drive around for mile after cursed mile before stopping so that his wife can ask for directions, and then he'll insist that he had been taking the scenic route. Or he'll pull an all-nighter as he futilely tries to assemble the 649-piece Hot Wheels racetrack that he gave little Johnny for Christmas, all the while refusing to consult the instructions because that's for wimps.

The only time a man feels comfortable seeking advice is when he's in a hardware store. And not a behemoth, faceless chain store, like The Home Depot or Lowe's, where everyone seems slightly dazed and confused by the furious flow of traffic. We're talking about the local hardware store.

It's a place where a man is greeted by a friendly chime as he opens the door and can look upon an ever-present herd of his own kind. He can walk to the counter with his head held high, point to the broken object he's holding, and ask a seasoned pro (whom he knows on a first-name basis), "Ya got one of these in stock?" As he poses the question, it matters little that he has no idea what "one of these" is. A man doesn't have to explain himself or acknowledge his inadequacies when he's in the hardware store. There aren't any judgments, raised eyebrows, or snarky comments—just quick answers and quick solutions.

But times are changing; the hardware store is no longer strictly the domain of men. A 2008 article in the *Wall Street Journal,* titled "Ms. Fix-It," describes how this bastion of maledom is being invaded by females—and not just the scantily clothed kind who are on the promotional calendars that are tacked to the store's walls. "These women," the article says, "are not only gung-ho about buying a home on their own dime; they're ready to lay the tile and patch the drywall too."

What's a guy to do? If women take over the local hardware store, there will be no place he can go to unabashedly ask, "Where can I find some nuts?"

Q Do New Year's resolutions work?

A John Norcross, a University of Scranton psychologist who has done several studies on the matter, found that slightly more than 40 percent of people stick to their New Year's resolutions for at least six months.

This sounds pretty good until you consider that it all depends on the resolution. For instance, if a bunch of people resolve to work out three times a week and 40 percent of them stick to it for six months, that's pretty good. But if they resolve to stop stealing stuff

out of their neighbors' garages and only 40 percent succeed, you'd want to steer clear of that cul-de-sac.

But we digress—we've strayed from our resolution to remain on topic this year. Norcross says that New Year's resolutions work ten times better than resolutions made at other times of the year. However, his contention stands in contrast to the feeling of some experts that New Year's resolutions are shaky because many people make them simply out of tradition and not because they're deeply motivated by real-life issues.

Two other recent studies—one sponsored by the U.S. government (yes, your tax dollars hard at work again) and the other headed by Richard Wiseman, a professor at the University of Hertfordshire in England—found that 12 percent of "resolvers" stick to their goals for a full year. Experts maintain that the more resolutions you make, the less chance there is that any of them will work. They also say that men have a better chance when they choose resolutions that can yield weekly progress (such as weight loss) and that women do better when they publicize their resolutions and enlist the help of friends and family.

Either way, success is far from certain. But, hey, even if your resolution fails, at least you can try again the following New Year's.

Q What's up with the Christmas stocking?

A When you think about it, many Christmas traditions are a bit, well, weird. And in these cynical, hyper-paranoid times, it's perhaps surprising that some of them still exist. Wastefully chopping down pine trees that will be decorated and displayed in our living rooms? Putting out milk and cookies to invite a "jolly" fat man into our homes while our children sleep? Gathering around something called a yule log? No, if Christmas were founded today, things would be different. The one tradition that might stand a chance, though, is as benign as it is bewildering: the hanging of the Christmas stocking.

There are several competing stories regarding the origin of the Christmas stocking. The most popular holds that the practice began with Saint Nicholas, who lived in the third and fourth centuries. There are a couple of versions of this origin. In one, Saint Nick assisted the poor of Italy by traipsing about the land on horseback and tossing long, knitted purses that were filled with coins and gifts through the open windows of the poverty-stricken.

The other, more fanciful account focuses on how Saint Nicholas helped a poor man and his three lovely daughters. As was the case with all lovely daughters back in the days of folklore, these three girls desired nothing more than to get married. Unfortunately, their destitute father had no money for a dowry. Saint Nick, upon hearing of this man's plight, decided to help. Wanting to remain anonymous, Nicholas rode past the home of the poor man three times during the night and tossed gold coins into an open window. By happy coincidence, there were stockings or shoes left by the fireplace to dry, and the coins fell into them. The girls found the coins, and they were soon married.

Another story—one that's far less interesting—states that the tradition started in Germany, where children would hang their stockings to dry near the fireplace. And legend has it that in Holland, children would leave their wooden shoes near the fireplace, filled with straw for Santa's reindeer; Santa, appreciative of the gesture, deposited gifts in the shoes.

Regardless of its origins, we know that the tradition is old: In an 1883 editorial in the *New York Times,* a writer lamented the relatively new custom of putting up Christmas trees and how it threatened to extinguish the older tradition of hanging up stockings. Ultimately, it doesn't really matter how or why these festive stockings came to be—just as long as they're full on Christmas morning.

Q Why are fraternity and sorority names strings of Greek letters?

A Believe it or not, the tradition didn't begin as an elaborate pretense for the revealing fun of coed toga parties. Far from it.

In 1776, five super-nerds at the College of William & Mary founded a secret society called Phi Beta Kappa to offer an outlet for the sort of open intellectual discussion that they believed was impossible to have in the classroom. They dedicated their society to the pursuit of learning and intellectual fellowship, which were the ideals of classical Greek thought. They named their society *Philosophia Biou Kubernetes,* a Greek slogan that translates to this: "Love of learning is the guide of life." As part of the spirit of secrecy, they referred to the society only by its Greek initials.

After the Revolutionary War, Phi Beta Kappa established chapters at other universities, extending its reach and reputation. In the

1820s, a new wave of semi-secret college clubs popped up in the Northeast, and they borrowed Phi Beta Kappa's Greek naming system. But the public soured on secret societies in 1826, when members of the Freemasons—the most infamous club society of all—were implicated in the disappearance of a disaffected member who had threatened them with public exposure. In the ensuing backlash against secret societies, Phi Beta Kappa and other collegiate groups decided to position themselves as open, university-sanctioned institutions, which paved the way for the fraternities and sororities of today.

Phi Beta Kappa has stuck to its square roots over the years. Today, it operates as a by-invitation-only honor society, not a fraternity. Meanwhile, many of the groups that it originally inspired now pay homage to the ancient Greeks' more sordid, booze-guzzling side. But at least the names are always classy.

Q Why do we cross our fingers for luck?

A Humans are a superstitious bunch. We won't walk under ladders. We avoid black cats. We greet Friday the thirteenth with fear and trepidation. And when we need an extra jolt of good luck—when, say, we're confronted with a ladder, a black cat, or Friday the thirteenth—we cross our fingers. Why?

Tradition connects the gesture to the Christian sign of the cross. In earlier times, people saw supernatural evil just about everywhere they looked. They often attributed illness and misfortune to the influences of evil forces, and they expected to find spirits, witches, and other supernatural pests lurking around every corner. When they stumbled upon evil, it was common practice to call on divine protection by making the sign of the cross (touching the forehead, then the chest, then the left and right shoulders in turn).

It's possible that crossed fingers were originally meant as a similar appeal for God's protection. By subtly forming a cross with the index and middle fingers, a frightened Christian wouldn't attract undue attention. After all, you wouldn't want the neighborhood witch to know you were on to her—she might turn you into a mule or dispatch gophers to ravage your garden.

It's possible that finger crossing predates the symbolism of the Christian cross. Some New Age spiritualists trace the gesture to a pagan practice in which two people would form a cross with each other's index fingers and then make a wish. In this case, the crossed fingers would have probably evoked the solar cross, an astrological sign that features an equilateral cross inside a ring and dates back to prehistoric times.

The solar cross was, among other things, associated with nature, earth, the sun, and divinity. According to this line of thinking, pagans believed that good spirits existed at the center of a perfect cross and that they could trap a wish there by making a cross with their fingers.

The practice of finger crossing continues to this day, even if we talk about it more than we actually do it. In fact, the phrase "keep your fingers crossed" dates back only to the 1920s. Even with the major strides we've made in understanding the universe around us, we remain, apparently, every bit as superstitious as our ancient ancestors were.

Q Why do sisters like to wear each other's clothes?

A What's better than getting a Betsey Johnson dress on sale? Getting it for free! Having a sister is like having instant access to a 24/7 designer rack sale in which everything is 100 percent off. *Cha-ching!*

For girls who live together, it makes perfect fashion sense to swap, borrow, and sometimes steal each other's threads. Back in the old days, particularly the Great Depression, sisters sometimes shared clothing out of necessity. But in this age of walk-in closets and Carrie Bradshaw, sharing clothes is a whole different game. It's all about radically expanding your wardrobe options. Trying on a different style for the day. Getting something "new" without ever leaving the house or spending a cent.

Ever looked in the closet and thought, "I've got absolutely nothing to wear"? Not when you've got a sister, whether she's a blood relation or a fashionable soul sister. Even Hollywood celebrities—those notorious clotheshorses who can't endure the embarrassment of appearing in the same outfit twice—are in on the

swap. When actress Naomi Watts couldn't find the right dress to wear to a swank Hollywood party, a yellow flower-print Prada went out on loan from the wardrobe of her gal pal, Nicole Kidman.

Of course, not all sisters are keen on this kind of wide-open closet policy. Some of us have little sisters who simply can't be trusted with anything Gap, let alone Donna Karan or Gucci. And then there are "big" sisters who have no business squeezing into those size twenty-seven Seven jeans—though they'll try to do so anyway. Got a sister who works behind the counter at a fast-food restaurant? If so, everything—and we mean everything—is absolutely off-limits. Who wants her favorite fuchsia cardigan returned unwashed and smelling of French fry oil? Wendy's is no place for angora.

This might not stop your stealthy sibs from helping themselves to your stuff anyway. As Australian poet Pam Brown put it: "If your sister is in a tearing hurry to go out and cannot catch your eye, she's wearing your best sweater."

Q Who dreamed up the bachelor party?

A Maybe you're a conspiracy theorist, and you think that a young bride-to-be came up with the idea as a way of getting the upper hand before the marriage was even consummated. It would be a clever ploy, setting up the groom for trouble and forcing him into months of repentance right off the bat.

But in his book *Bachelor Party Confidential: A Real-Life Peek Behind the Closed-Door Tradition,* David Boyer traces the dawn of the bachelor party to about 500 BC, when soldiers in ancient Sparta would gather for lavish dinners, during which the guests exchanged toasts and the groom-to-be reiterated his commitment to his fellow men.

Boyer says that it's difficult to pin down exactly when the racier elements of today's bachelor parties began to creep into the festivities, but he notes that a high-society bachelor bash in New York City in 1896 was raided by the police, who had reason to believe that naked women were part of the entertainment. They were wrong—it was just a belly dancer. Nevertheless, the saucy shindig made headlines. The fact that the police had their suspicions suggests that even in those days, rowdies were getting away with the types of wild bachelor parties we've come to know and love today.

Boyer is the Studs Terkel of stag, relying on oral histories to show how the bachelor party evolved over the course of the twentieth century. While the parties were wild enough in the pre-World War II days, they were primarily the domain of the upper class. After the war, however, when returning servicemen were getting married en masse, the modern bachelor party—with its requisite booze, strippers, and various forms of insanity—became a true cultural phenomenon.

So the next time you wake up at sunrise in a pool of your own vomit after celebrating a buddy's impending marriage, take solace in the fact that you've merely been carrying on a noble tradition that was started by the Spartan soldiers.

Q Why do we put candles on a birthday cake?

A Are we feeling a little sensitive about the five-alarm fire that is blazing atop the buttercream frosting? Well, take heart—

the tradition of lighting candles on cakes is way older than you. The custom dates back to the ancient Greeks.

It all began as an offering to Artemis, goddess of the moon. The Greeks baked round honey cakes, topped them with tapers, and placed them on the altar of Artemis's temple. When lit, the round cakes looked like—you guessed it—full, glowing moons. Back then, people believed that smoke carried their thoughts up to the gods (hence, all of the sacrificial fires). These days, we associate lighting and blowing out the candles with making a wish. But just when did candle-topped cakes become an essential part of the party?

Many historians trace the modern use of candles on cakes to Kinderfest, a German birthday celebration for children that dates to the fifteenth century. In those days, people believed that children were particularly susceptible to evil spirits on their birthdays, so friends and family gathered around protectively, lighting candles on a cake to carry good wishes up to God. It was customary for the candles to remain lit all day, and the cake was served after the evening meal.

By the eighteenth century, birthday cakes and candles took on a more festive feel. The research of culinary historian Shirley Cherkasky points to a 1799 letter written by Johann Wolfgang von Goethe (one of the greatest figures of world literature) that recounts his fiftieth birthday: "When it was time for dessert, the prince's entire livery in full regalia entered, led by the major-domo. He carried a generous-size torte with colorful flaming candles—amounting to some fifty candles—that began to melt and threatened to burn down, instead of there being enough room for candles indicating upcoming years."

Well, what do you know? You and Goethe actually have something in common: birthday cakes that resemble towering infernos. But, hey, controlled fires can be really fun (just ask any pyromaniac). And perhaps that's why the German birthday cake tradition eventually made its way over to the United States. As an 1889 American style guide directed: "At birthday parties, the birthday cake, with as many tiny colored candles set about its edge as the child is years old, is, of course, of special importance."

By 1921, American candle manufacturers started advertising boxes of little candles in mixed colors. And a few years later, people all over the United States could order cake candles and candle holders from the famous Sears Roebuck catalog. But you're way too young to remember that. Right?

Chapter Five

FOOD AND DRINK

Q Can man live on bread alone?

A When the economy began heading south in 2008, we here at F.Y.I. headquarters were forced to make some difficult changes. Gone were the in-house massage therapist and the mariachi band. Worst of all, gone were our catered meals. Instead of the champagne fountain, we had a rusty faucet; instead of sashimi and caviar, our break-room larders were stocked with loaves of month-old Wonder Bread. (If you've noticed a decline in the quality of these articles, you now know why.) Naturally, we began to ponder the following question: Would we be able to survive on a diet of Wonder Bread and water?

First we had to figure out just how much Wonder Bread would be required for us to make it through a typical day. Wonder Bread contains about sixty calories per slice, with about twenty-two slices to a loaf. Considering that the United States Department of Agriculture recommends that the average human eat about two thousand calories per day, we would have had to chow down on more than a loaf and a half of bread per day merely to satisfy our caloric requirements. But caloric intake was far from our biggest concern. As Deuteronomy tells us, "And he humbled thee, and suffered thee to hunger, and fed thee with manna, which thou knewest not, neither did thy fathers know; that he might make thee know that man doth not live by bread only, but by every *word* that proceedeth out of the mouth of the Lord doth man live."

Okay, we're not sure what that last bit means. But we do know this: No number of words proceedething from anyone's mouth is going to help if bread is the last brick standing in a crumbled food pyramid. That's because bread is lacking in crucial vitamins and minerals, particularly vitamins A and C.

On the bright side, Wonder Bread has zero cholesterol, which meant that we probably weren't going to die of a heart attack. However, our cholesterol levels were the least of our problems. Vitamin A deficiency leads to a number of problems, including blindness, which was going to make it tough to edit this book. What's more, a lack of vitamin C leads to scurvy, a really nasty disease whose early symptoms include teeth falling out.

Ultimately, our bodies wouldn't have been able to withstand the dearth of essential nutrients; within months, we would have been dead. Even though we wound up ditching our "bread alone" plan, it might explain why our bosses rushed us to finish this book.

Q Whatever happened to the lunchbox?

A Between 1950 and 1970, approximately one hundred and twenty million lunchboxes were sold in the United States—an astounding total that amounted to one and a half lunchboxes for every boy and girl born in the baby-boom generation. So just what happened to those kitschy lunch containers that were emblazoned with the likes of Bobby Sherman, Roy Rogers, G.I. Joe, Superman, and the Jetsons? You can blame their demise on heavy metal.

Sales of lunchboxes first began to slow in the early 1970s, which was right around the time that the product's manufacturers made the switch from metal to molded plastic. The new plastic cases were clearly inferior to the original metal ones in durability (and pizzazz), but the manufacturers went this route to cut costs—and to appease some overprotective mothers.

Kids will be kids, and back in the good old days, they found that their metal lunch containers could be used for purposes other than toting PB&J and bologna. These included bullying and bashing other kids in the head. "No, I will not trade you my Twinkies for your pretzels." *Bam-o!*

Concerned with the safety of their children, many parents lobbied for the ban of metal lunchboxes. In Florida, the legislature went so far as to rule metal lunchboxes "lethal weapons." The last lunchbox of the steel age rolled off the Thermos production line in 1987. Somewhat apropos, it featured a heavily armed Sylvester Stallone as Rambo.

These days, kids buy lunch, brown-bag it, or carry some kind of soft-sided lunch tote with superior foam insulation. Sure, everything inside that tote may stay cold, but it'll never be as cool as a 1977 metal lunchbox featuring KISS.

Q What is the 7 in 7-Up?

A We'll never know for sure. The soft drink's creator, Charles Leiper Grigg, went to the grave without revealing where he got the name. But there are several interesting rumors regarding its origin.

When Grigg introduced his drink in October 1929, it had neither a "7" nor an "Up" in its name. He called it Bib-Label Lithiated Lemon-Lime Soda. (Imagine trying to order that bad boy at the Taco Bell drive-thru.) "Bib-Label" referred to the use of paper labels that were placed on plain bottles, and "Lithiated" related to the mood-altering drug lithium.

Despite having a bizarre name, hitting store shelves two weeks before the stock market crashed, and facing competition from about six hundred other lemon-lime sodas, the new drink sold pretty well. (Chalk it up to the cool, refreshing taste of lithium.) But even with the success, Grigg soon realized that Bib-Label Lithiated Lemon-Lime Soda was a little tricky to remember (or maybe he just got sick of saying it himself), so he changed the name to 7-Up.

Here's the most pervasive (and logical) explanation for the name: The "7" refers to the drink's seven ingredients, and the "Up" has to do with the soda's rising bubbles. This version is supported by an early 7-Up tagline: "Seven natural flavors blended into a savory, flavory drink with a real wallop." The seven ingredients were carbonated water, sugar, citric acid, lithium citrate, sodium citrate, and essences of lemon and lime oils (technically two ingredients). Of course, it's entirely possible that ad executives devised the ingredients angle to fit the name rather than vice versa.

There are other possible origins, but these theories range from the unlikely to the preposterous. It's quite possible that the "7" refers to nothing at all—Grigg may have simply devised an enigmatic name to pique people's interest. In any case, the name seemed to work out okay. By 1940, 7-Up was the third-best-selling soft drink in the world. And even when delicious lithium was dropped from the recipe in 1950, the drink remained a hit.

Q Who's Mary, and how'd she get so bloody?

A If you're a student of history, you'll know that "Bloody Mary" is the nickname that was given to Mary Tudor. As the first queen to rule England (1553–1558), Mary Tudor is best remembered for the brutality of her effort to re-establish Catholicism as the religion of the state. (She was trying to undo the change that her father, Henry VIII, had made when he dissed the pope, divorced Mary's mother, and got hitched—if we can believe Hollywood—to Natalie Portman.) Mary Tudor's plan involved hanging non-Catholics, rebels, and heretics from the gibbet and burning nearly three hundred others at the stake. It's little wonder that she was given such an unpleasant moniker.

But for those of us who are less historically minded, the words "Bloody Mary" conjure a much more pleasant image: no roasting of Protestants, just a delicious glass of spicy tomato juice and vodka. So how did such a terrifying monarch inspire such a tasty drink?

It seems that the name of this popular barroom beverage has been connected to a number of historical and fictional women. By most popular accounts, the Bloody Mary was indeed named for Mary I, England's royal slaughteress. However, others associate the Bloody Mary with everyone from Hollywood actress Mary Pickford to the beheaded Mary, Queen of Scots, to Mary Worth (according to an urban legend, a child-murdering witch who will scratch your eyes out when summoned to your bathroom mirror).

The truth is, the Bloody Mary's creator, Fernand Petiot, had none of these women in mind when he concocted the original tomato juice and vodka cocktail at Harry's New York Bar in Paris in the 1920s. Petiot said, "One of the boys suggested we call the drink 'Bloody Mary' because it reminded him of the Bucket of Blood Club in Chicago, and a girl there named Mary."

Interestingly, when Petiot moved from his post in Paris to the King Cole Bar at the St. Regis in New York in 1934, the hotel tried to change the name of his Bloody Mary to Red Snapper (the term "bloody" was considered a tad rude in certain sophisticated circles), but the new name never stuck. Over time, Petiot modified the drink, spicing it up with black and cayenne pepper, Worcestershire sauce, lemon, and Tabasco sauce.

Today, more than a million Bloody Marys are served every day in the United States. Whether garnished with a celery stick, pickle, lemon, or lime, one thing's for sure: This blood-red cocktail is bloody good. Cheers to you, Mary.

Q How do they salt peanuts in the shell?

A No, bioengineers haven't created a super breed of naturally salty peanut plants (yet). The real answer isn't nearly as exciting.

To salt peanuts while they're still in the shell, food manufacturers soak them in brine (salty water). In one typical approach, the first step is to treat the peanuts with a wetting agent—a chemical compound that reduces surface tension in water, making it penetrate the shell more readily. Next, the peanuts are placed into an enclosed metal basket and immersed in an airtight pressure vessel that is filled with brine. The pressure vessel is then depressurized to drive air out of the peanut shells and suck in saltwater.

Peanuts may go through several rounds of pressurization and depressurization. Once the peanuts are suitably salty, they are rinsed with clean water and spun on a centrifuge in order to get rid of the bulk of the water. Finally, they are popped into an oven so that the drying process can be completed.

Now, if they could just figure out how to cram some chocolate in those peanuts.

Q Does Heinz really make fifty-seven different sauces?

A In our opinion—actually, in the opinion of most reasonable, intelligent humans—ketchup is a miracle sauce. It's a modern-day Balm of Gilead that not only heals all culinary wounds, but turns everything it touches into something really, really delicious. We can't help but notice, though, that each time we take out a bottle of Heinz ketchup to douse our plate, the little label near the neck promises another fifty-six varieties of this magical substance. Could it be?

Sadly, no. In fact, there's only one type of ketchup—tomato. But ketchup isn't the only item that Heinz makes. Henry J. Heinz didn't even get his start in the condiment industry by selling ketchup. Born in 1844 in Pittsburgh, Heinz began his food-sales career as a preteen, hawking vegetables that he grew himself.

Later, in his spare time from his job managing the family brick-making business, Heinz began selling prepared horseradish door to door. He didn't get into the ketchup game until 1876, by which time he'd already built a relatively large condiments business selling horseradish, pickles, and sauerkraut (hey, he was in Pittsburgh).

In 1896, Heinz struck upon his famous slogan. Unlike Heinz's delicious, delicious ketchup, the story behind the slogan's conception is rather bland. As Heinz was riding an elevated train in New York City, he noticed an advertisement for a shoe store offering "21 styles" of shoes. For reasons unexplained, Heinz was captivated by this rather mundane advertisement and, soon after, decided upon the now-famous "57 varieties" motto.

There is no definitive explanation for why H. J. chose that number. At the time, he was not offering fifty-seven sauce varieties, though he was peddling more than sixty kinds of food, including something called "euchred pickles." (We've played euchre while pickled, but we have no idea what euchred pickles are.) Despite the banality of the slogan, it seemed to resonate: By the early nineteen hundreds, the Heinz company was far and away the most popular purveyor of condiments and prepared sauces.

Nowadays the Heinz company sells well more than a thousand products, ranging from baby food to barbecue sauce. Of course, only one of these products really matters—and all God-loving Americans know what it is.

This leads us to another pressing question: What's the difference between catsup and ketchup? The answer: Nothing, really.

Q How did the cocktail get its name?

A In *The Spy*, James Fennimore Cooper's 1821 novel about the American Revolution, secret agents and double agents reconnoiter in a smoky tavern that's overseen by an Irish woman named Betty Flanagan. In addition to her loyalty and courage,

"Betty," Cooper tells us, "had the merit of being the inventor of that beverage which is so well known at the present hour to all the patriots...and which is distinguished by the name of 'cock-tail.'"

Did an Irish barmaid in Westchester County, New York, really concoct the first cocktail around 1780? According to one legend, the cocktail does indeed go back to the days of the American Revolution. Supposedly, Continental soldiers and their French allies liked to kick back at local inns after a hard day of fighting off British redcoats. The Americans usually opted for a shot of whiskey or gin, while the suaver French preferred wine, sherry, or vermouth.

One evening, some soldiers decided that they wanted a little dinner—perhaps a bit of *coq au vin*—with their drinks, and they nabbed a few chickens and a rooster from a neighboring Tory farmer. In honor of the feast, they garnished their glasses with the rooster's plucked tail feathers and toasted each other. A great American institution—the cocktail hour—was born.

That's one story, anyway. Other explanations are somewhat more prosaic. "Cocktail" could be a Yankee corruption of *decota,* the Latin word for "distilled water." Or it could come from New Orleans, where an eggcup called a "coquetier" was used to measure out liquor. Or it could have originated even farther south, in Latin America, where native people used a root from a plant the Spanish called the *cola de gallo* ("cock's tail") to stir fermented beverages.

The first printed definition of cocktail appeared on May 13, 1806, in the Hudson, New York, newspaper *The Balance and Colombian*

Repository: "Cock-tail, then, is a stimulating liquor composed of spirits of any kind, sugar, water, and bitters." With an occasional dash of politics, too, for the editor noted, "[It] is supposed to be an excellent electioneering potion...because, a person having swallowed a glass of it, is ready to swallow anything else."

There seem to be as many theories about the genesis of the cocktail as there are variations on the drink itself. One thing most historians agree on, however, is that cocktails are a uniquely American innovation. "Professor" Jerry Thomas, who is often hailed as the father of American mixology, included dozens of cocktail recipes in his 1862 bartender's guide *How to Mix Drinks.* He offered brandy, gin, champagne, whiskey, and rum cocktails, both plain and fancy; a "Jersey Cocktail," made from hard cider; and an alcohol-free version with soda and a twist of lemon.

So drink up! No matter where the name comes from, cocktails are as American as apple pie and the Fourth of July. They're the perfect libation for our multicultural, mix-it-up nation.

Q Why do people put little umbrellas in their drinks?

A That pretty paper parasol may seem like nothing more than a froufrou-y finish to your mai tai or piña colada, but it once served a noble purpose.

Back in the early barroom days, hanging out at the neighborhood pub was pretty much a guys-only activity. What? Bars without women? Where in the world were men able to use their cheesy

pick-up lines? Believe it or not,
cocktail umbrellas helped to take
care of that conundrum.

In the early 1930s, bartenders at
swanky island-themed watering
holes like Trader Vic's and Don
the Beachcomber thought up a
clever little way to lure in the
ladies. They concocted all sorts of
fanciful cocktails and garnished
them with cute paper sunshades.
Sure it was a marketing ploy, but it worked. By the 1950s and
1960s, exotic decorated drinks and Polynesian-themed restaurants
and clubs became part of a whole tiki culture craze. From that
moment on, the ladies—and the umbrellas—were at the bar to
stay.

There are plenty of guys who enjoy refreshingly fruity umbrella
drinks from time to time, too. In an effort to defend their manhood, they may come up with more "technical" reasons for
covering their lava flows or zombies with a colorful little canopies.
Some maintain that cocktail umbrellas shade their icy, frothy, frap-
pés from the melting effects of solar radiation. Others suggest that
cocktail umbrellas prevent volatile alcohol molecules within their
drinks from evaporating too quickly.

Is this a bunch of hogwash, or do cocktail umbrellas really have
science on their side? Perhaps a little bit of science—but it's more
likely that these umbrellas simply evoke a sunny state of mind.
Every once in a while, we all need to ditch reality for that white
beach, where coconuts and pineapples and maraschino cherries

are ingredients in luscious libations that smell like suntan lotion—and somehow still taste really good.

Q Is breakfast really the most important meal of the day?

A If your idea of breakfast is a double martini, probably not. Otherwise, the answer is yes. Evidence suggests that kicking the day off with a reasonably healthy meal is one of the best things you can do for your body.

The clearest benefit to breakfast is that it helps to keep your metabolism humming along at the right rate. Why? If you go too long without eating, you risk triggering a starvation reflex in your body. We evolved to live in the wild, which means that our bodies don't know anything about dieting or rushing off to work or any of the other modern-day reasons for skipping meals. On a cellular level, not eating for a long period of time indicates to your body that there's no food around. As a precaution against potential starvation, your energy level drops and you start saving up energy in the form of fat.

Breakfast, then, is vital because when you wake up, you've already gone a long time without eating. Let's say that you have an evening snack at nine o'clock and then don't eat until lunchtime the next day. That's fifteen hours without food—plenty of time for glucose levels to fall and for your body to start preparing for a perceived dearth of food in the future. The upshot? You're more sluggish, and the calories that you consume at lunch probably produce more fat than they would otherwise. Even a healthy lunch might not get your glucose levels back to where they should be, so you may remain sluggish for the rest of the afternoon.

The consequences of skipping breakfast don't end there. In a Harvard Medical School study that was published in 2003, researchers found that people who skip breakfast are three times more likely to be obese than those who eat a meal first thing in the morning. Furthermore, they're twice as likely to develop problems with blood sugar, which can increase the risks of diabetes and heart disease.

Of course, not all breakfasts are created equal. Research suggests that the best bet is to eat relatively small portions that contain low-fat complex carbohydrates (like whole grain cereal) and a little protein (yogurt or milk). Sugary breakfasts (doughnuts, kids' cereals) can lead to energy crashes later in the day, and heavy meals that are high in fat (the "everything" omelet at Frank's Diner) can make you feel sluggish. In other words, breakfast is only important if you do it up right.

Chapter Six

ANIMAL KINGDOM

Q Which are smarter, dogs or cats?

A Until either a dog or a cat develops a cure for cancer, we can't settle this ongoing debate. The concept of intelligence is too nebulous, and dogs and cats are too different from one another. Furthermore, most people—whether they own a cat or a dog—are convinced that their little wookums is the most amazing pet in the world, and no one can tell them otherwise.

The biggest obstacle in crowning an ultimate pet genius is that cats and dogs have contrasting goals. Dogs evolved as pack animals—their ancestors hunted in groups—so they are highly social. Dogs are hardwired to pick up signals and understand commands, and they are driven to please their pack leaders. These days, those pack leaders tend to be humans, which helps explain why canines are so easily trained.

Cats, on the other hand, evolved to hunt alone; consequently, they're motivated to take care of themselves. Most felines exhibit remarkable intelligence when it comes to self-preservation and self-reliance. They're extremely skilled at mapping out their surroundings: They can travel long distances, escape from tight spaces, and pull off spectacular leaping, balancing, and landing maneuvers.

If you define intelligence broadly—as the mastery of complex skills—there's a good case to be made for both dogs and cats. But if you define intelligence the way we do in school—as the ability to absorb information and then utilize this data when tested—dogs appear to be at the head of the class.

In experiments in which animals are rewarded for figuring out complex tasks (like hitting levers or navigating a maze), dogs invariably outperform cats. Dogs have learned to do things that cats can't come close to doing, like distinguishing photos of different dog breeds and even human faces. The evidence suggests that dogs also possess greater language abilities. Some dogs understand well more than two hundred words or signals; this is roughly the equivalent of a two-year-old human's vocabulary. Cats, meanwhile, seem to top out at approximately fifty words, which is about the same comprehension that an eighteen-month-old human displays.

But the evidence might be misleading—dogs are more innately driven to perform in order to earn praise and treats. It's difficult to motivate cats to do anything in experiments because they're so independent. And language is a social ability, so it's more suited to a pack animal like a dog.

The counter argument is that cats could master the same skills as dogs, but they're smart enough not to bother. Why bust your butt if you can lounge around while someone feeds and shelters you? Doesn't this mean that cats are smarter than their *owners,* too? Most cat owners have long suspected as much.

Q Why don't we ride zebras?

A What's black, white, and red? A zebra enraged at the thought of someone riding on its back.

While the zebra belongs to the horse family, it is kind of like the deranged cousin nobody likes: He gets invited to Thanksgiving out of a sense of familial obligation, but everybody hopes he'll have other plans. It's inevitable that he'll have a few too many drinks, get all emotional, and then start an argument that leaves everyone avoiding eye contact and thinking up lame excuses for going home early.

Domesticating a zebra is a dicey proposition, though it's been done. For example, it's a real zebra that Hayden Panettiere rides in the 2005 movie *Racing Stripes,* which is about a zebra that aspires to be a racehorse. But the average zebra is far more temperamental than a horse. Zebras spook easily, and they can be exceptionally irritable, especially as they get older. One zebra trainer compared riding the ill-humored beast to "riding a coiled spring."

There have been attempts to create zebra hybrids, such as a "zorse" (a cross between a zebra and a horse) or a "zonkey" (a cross between a zebra and a donkey). But because zebras don't have any particularly useful qualities, such as speed or strength, these hybrids don't have real-world utility beyond the chuckles their whimsical names might elicit.

If you really have a strong urge to "ride a zebra," your best bet might be to head down to the local high school and harass the referees at the football and basketball games. Those zebras may be just as temperamental as the real ones, but they're less likely to kick you in the face.

Q Why is a dog man's best friend?

A Tales of dogs' loyalty to their human companions are legion. One famous story involves Hachiko, a dog in Tokyo whose master died at work one day. Hachiko spent most of the rest of his life—about ten years—waiting obediently at the Shibuya train station, hoping for his master's return.

We've all heard anecdotes about dogs who were lost many miles from home but found their way back. Perhaps you have your own story about a lovable mutt who greets you at the door each evening with an unbridled enthusiasm that suggests he feared he might never see you again after you left that morning.

Dogs are more than just pets. They serve as faithful helpers to farmers, hunters, the police, and the disabled, among others. In ancient Egypt, dogs were seen as sacred, and some even had their own servants. (Plenty of dog owners would tell you that tradition continues today.) No animal has been a better friend to humans—although in some Asian cultures, dogs are more closely associated with the word "fried" than "friend."

It's a friendship that began more than fifteen thousand years ago, when humans, probably in East Asia, began to domesticate gray wolves. Possessing speed, strength, and powerful senses of sight, smell, and hearing, these animals were valuable for hunting and protection. As human needs evolved, new breeds of dogs were created to address them.

Many people say that they have special bonds with their dogs—that Fido has a keen sense of when humans are happy, sad, or angry. Some recent scientific studies may back up such claims. Dogs seem to understand human behavioral cues better than other animals do, though it's not entirely clear which cues the dogs are interpreting. Your dog might be reacting to extremely subtle variations in your body language, such as the tilt of your head or the position of your arm.

So the next time a dog starts to get a little amorous with your leg, you can't necessarily blame him for bad behavior. It could be that he simply thought your shin was giving him a come-hither look.

Q Why does the sperm whale have such a dirty name?

A Basically, because whalers had dirty minds. The weirdest of the many weird parts of a sperm whale's anatomy is the spermaceti organ, a mass of oil-soaked spongy material that is located in the head and makes up about 25 to 33 percent of the entire animal. Because this substance has a milky-white appearance, whalers logically concluded that it was the whale's semen (which is what *spermaceti* literally means in Latin). The name stuck.

We know today that there isn't any sperm in a sperm whale's head, but the purpose of the spermaceti organ remains a mystery. One long-held belief is that it's a built-in battering ram for battling enemies and rivals. Another possibility is that it helps whales control their buoyancy, since oil is less dense than water.

But the most influential explanation suggests that the organ is involved in creating and focusing the sound waves that whales use for echolocation—the biological sonar that gives whales, dolphins, and bats the ability to "see" by bouncing sound waves off of the animals' surroundings. Some biologists believe that an air pulse travels through the spermaceti organ before rebounding off of a fatty cushion and out into the ocean through lens-like structures at the front of the whale's head. A bigger spermaceti organ, the theory goes, enables sperm whales to generate lower-frequency sounds, which can travel farther.

Hence, a giant spermaceti organ equals an expanded echolocation range. It's not as provocative as a head that's filled with sperm, but it's still pretty cool.

Q How many animals have yet to be discovered?

A Since about 1.3 million animal species around the planet have been identified and named, you might think that we're down to the last few undiscovered critters by now.

But according to many biologists, we're probably not even 10 percent of the way there. In fact, experts estimate that the planet holds ten million to one hundred million undiscovered plant and animal species, excluding single-celled organisms like bacteria and algae. This estimate is based on the number of species found in examined environments and on the sizes of the areas we have yet to fully investigate.

The broad span of the estimate shows just how little we know about life on Earth. At the heart of the mystery are the oceans and tropical rain forests. More than 70 percent of the planet is underwater. We know that the oceans teem with life, but we've explored only a small fraction of them. The watery realm is like an entire planet unto itself. Biologists haven't examined much of the tropical rain forests, either, but the regions that they have explored have turned up a dizzying variety of life. It's hard to say exactly how many life forms have yet to be discovered, but the majority probably are small invertebrates (animals without backbones).

Insects make up the vast majority of the animal kingdom. There are about nine hundred thousand known varieties, and this number will probably increase significantly as we further explore the rain forests. Terry Erwin is an influential coleopterist—in other words, a beetle guy—who estimated that the tropics alone could contain thirty million separate insect and arthropod species. This number is based on his examination of forest canopies in South America and Central America, and it suggests that you're on the wrong planet if you hate bugs.

Cataloging all these critters is slow-going. It requires special knowledge to distinguish between similar insect species and to identify different ocean species. It also takes real expertise to know which animals are already on the books and which are not. Qualified experts are in short supply, and they have a lot on their plates.

In some respects, time is of the essence. Deforestation and climate change are killing off animal and plant species even before they've been discovered. You may not particularly care about wildlife, but these are big losses. The knowledge gained from some of these undiscovered creatures that are on death row could help to cure diseases and, thus, make the world a better place.

Q Do insects ever get fat?

A It's not surprising that you don't see any obese insects ambling around your yard. If you existed on a diet of leaves, garbage, and rotting corpses, would *you* overeat? But as it turns out, insects can't get fat even if they want to—their bodies won't allow it.

Insects (as well as other arthropods, such as spiders, scorpions, and crustaceans) have exoskeletons—rigid outer body parts that are made of chitin and other material—instead of internal skeletons like humans have. The hard stuff is all on the outside, while the fat and other squishy stuff is all on the inside. The only way for an insect to get bigger is to molt, which involves forming a new exoskeleton underneath the old one and casting off the old material.

Some species start off as smaller versions of full-grown adults and go through progressive molts until they reach their full sizes. Others start off in larval stages, grow steadily, and then enter pupal stages so that they can metamorphose into adults. (For example, a caterpillar forms a cocoon and turns into a butterfly or moth.) If an insect eats a lot while it's still growing, it will simply molt sooner rather than get chunky.

Were an insect to overeat after reaching full maturity, the fat wouldn't have anywhere to go because the exoskeleton is rigid. The results would be catastrophic. Researchers learned this by severing the stomach nerves of flies, so that the flies couldn't sense that they had had their fill. The flies kept feeding until they burst open.

Bugs have an innate sense of exactly how much sustenance they need. There's evidence that insects adapt their metabolisms over multiple generations, depending on how much food is in their environments. A study published in 2006 showed that diamond-back moth caterpillars that lived in carbohydrate-rich environments going back eight generations could load up on more carbs without adding fat than could caterpillars that had evolved in carbohydrate-poor environments over the same time period.

The study could be a sign that other animals, including humans, will evolve metabolic adaptations based on the food in their environments. This doesn't help us much today, but if we start pounding Whoppers, nachos, and Big Macs now, perhaps our descendants will be able to scarf them down without gaining a single pound.

Q Which animal has the largest penis?

A Does size matter? Countless magazines have been sold promising to answer this question once and for all. And email spammers certainly have their opinions—thus, the barrage of unsolicited messages that read, "It's better to be gigantic than romantic" or "Big penis, you can have it." Those spammers might be on to something. But a trip through the animal kingdom can still make the well-endowed man envious—and give the man with humble gifts a reason to stand tall.

Reportedly, the largest penis on record belongs to a New Yorker named Jonah Cardeli Falcon—it measures 13.5 inches long when erect and 9.5 inches in a relaxed state. This might sound impressive, but consider that the mighty blue whale has been found to be packing anywhere from five to eight *feet* of whalehood. This shouldn't be a surprise; the blue whale is the world's largest animal in every sense, with a body that's typically ninety to one hundred feet long.

However, the blue whale's penis-size advantage becomes much less impressive when you bring proportions into the mix. An eight-foot penis on a one-hundred-foot blue whale is roughly equivalent to a ten-centimeter penis on a human. That's hardly the stuff of legends.

No, the real "oohs" and "ahs" should be reserved for the Argentine blue-bill, a small, stiff-tailed duck—the jokes begin to write themselves—whose body averages about sixteen inches in length. One specimen of this species was found to have a flaccid penis of almost seventeen inches coiled inside its cloaca (the cavity into which the intestinal, urinary, and generative canals open in birds). Proportionally speaking, if that duck had instead been a six-foot-tall man, he would have had a six-foot penis. Now, that would really sell some magazines.

Q Why does a dog walk in a circle before lying down?

A Inside every dog is a wolf. Whether the dog is big or small, vicious or just-as-sweet-as-can-be—it doesn't matter. These are animals that are descended from wolves, and somewhere in the recesses of their DNA, certain behaviors are encoded and may never peter out. Turning around before lying down is thought to be one.

Dog experts believe that canines walk in circles before lying down because they're unconsciously recalling the nights their ancestors spent in the wilderness. Wolves don't have the luxury of sleeping on quilted pads or at the foot of a kind master's bed; they sleep whenever and wherever the impulse takes them. This might be in an area overgrown with tough grasses, ferns, and other plants, so they make a few circles in order to trample the undergrowth. It may not be as comfortable as a plush carpet or a padded area rug, but at least the wolf can ensure that it won't get poked in the rear end by a sharp stem.

Another plausible explanation along the same line has to do with creepy-crawlies. In the wilderness, there's a chance that a snake or an equally unpleasant creature will have already settled into the spot that a wolf has chosen for its nap. The circling may be intended to flush out such critters.

Sure, Fido isn't going to encounter any snakes at the foot of your bed—but old habits seem to die hard.

Q Why is bird poop white?

A Since a typical bird dines mainly on worms, bugs, and assorted garbage, it seems logical that it would poop in hues of brown, like the rest of us. What's going on? Do birds take special white-poo supplements just to maximize their car-defacing potential? No. Bird poop is, in fact, brown. The white stuff is urine—and this leads us to a sophisticated discussion about the differences between pee and poop.

You pee to eliminate excess water and waste products that result from cell metabolism. Essentially, the cells in your body do what they do through chemical processes that use the oxygen you breathe and chemical compounds derived from the food you eat. These chemical processes result in new, leftover chemical compounds that your body needs to expel. You eliminate one of the biggies—carbon dioxide—through breathing. You eliminate everything else through sweating and peeing. Poop, on the other hand, is food that your body didn't need in the first place. The body takes what's useful from the food that you eat, breaks it down into sugars and proteins your cells can use, and sends the rest on its way, as poop.

Among the primary metabolic waste products your body must get rid of are nitrogen compounds. These compounds are toxic to cells and would kill you if they remained in your body in their straight form. Your body needs to convert these toxic compounds into something safer en route to their excretion. Humans, other mammals, and amphibians do this by turning nitrogen compounds into a substance called urea, which can be dissolved into water. When converted to urea and added to water, the nitrogen is relatively harmless.

This doesn't work for reptiles and birds, however, because they lay eggs. A bird embryo that's inside a shell doesn't receive a steady supply of water, and since it has no place to keep all that urine anyway, urea won't do the trick. Instead, reptiles and birds convert their waste into uric acid—white crystals that form a pasty solid, which a bird embryo can safely have inside the egg until it's hatched. The uric-acid excretion process means that birds and reptiles don't have to drink much water—they need just a bit of it to excrete the urea.

In birds, poop proper comes out the same hole as the uric acid waste, so most droppings are a mixture of the white uric acid and brown material. And that, fair reader, is why the stuff that's cling-ing so stubbornly to your car's windshield looks the way it does.

Q Which animal is the smartest?

A This one's a no-brainer: *Homo sapiens.* Not to toot our own horn, but human beings set the bar for intelligence and higher-level thinking.

As for non-humans, the dispute is ongoing over what constitutes intelligence in animals. Some believe that there are four basic qualifications for animal intelligence: use of tools, problem solv-ing, communication, and self-awareness. Many species exhibit one or two of these traits; some researchers believe that the three species we're about to discuss exhibit all four.

Our genetic cousins, the great apes, reside at the top of just about every list of intelligent animals. Apes can communicate not only with each other, but also with their human caretakers. Koko, a lowland gorilla famous for her mastery of sign language, has developed a vocabulary of more than one thousand signs in nearly forty years of instruction. Koko was born in 1971 in the San Francisco Zoo, and she currently resides at The Gorilla Foundation in Woodside, California. She has taught scientists a great deal about the intelligence of gorillas: In addition to her amazing grasp of language, she is able to express thoughts and emotions.

The dolphin possesses levels of intelligence that are similar to those of the great ape; the dolphin, though, seems less serious-minded. You might call dolphins the artists of the animal kingdom: Experts have gone so far as to say that they possess a kind of creativity. Dolphins frolic more than any other species, actively and frequently engaging in activities that have nothing to do with survival. They also are among the few animals on the planet to recognize that sex is good for more than just making babies.

If apes are chatty and dolphins are artistic, elephants are emphatic. Elephants have been observed grieving for lost relatives and exhibiting comforting behavior toward other mourners. With their legendary memories, elephants develop a familiarity with other animals and with humans that runs deeper than most interspecies relationships.

Elephants can also solve simple problems. For instance, the 1950 book *Elephant Bill,* written by J. H. Williams, describes domestic elephants in Burma that were fitted with collars and bells. The crafty beasts were found to be clogging the bells with mud in order to sneak into a local banana grove for late-night snacks.

Now that's smart. Those elephants might not have had anything on Albert Einstein, but they would have at least given Homer Simpson a run for his money.

Q Why does a dog like to roll on its back?

A Your dog might look kind of silly as it rolls around on its back, but there's a method to the madness. Some experts suggest that a canine does this in order to replace its natural scent with another odor—it's an instinct that is thought to have been passed down through the generations as a form of camouflage. By concealing its odor, the dog has a better chance of sneaking up on prey.

This is why dogs sometimes roll in stuff that's pungent, such as feces, grass that has been urinated on, and even the carcasses of herbivores (although this is more common in wolves and hunting dogs than house dogs). The stronger the scent, the better. This does much to explain a dog's tendency to dirty itself just after a bath. A dog smells most like its natural self when it's clean, but a quick roll in the grass will solve that problem.

But as any dog owner knows, there are other reasons for these back-rolling shenanigans. A dog likes to have its stomach rubbed, and the best way for the animals to presents its tummy to its doting master is to roll on its back. According to animal behaviorists, this is a sign of a healthy relationship between the dog and its owner. When a dog exposes its soft, vulnerable underside in this manner, it means it trusts its master.

Of course, excessive rolling—especially when a certain part of its body is pinpointed—might mean that the dog has an itch that it can't scratch. In other words, your dog might have fleas or dermatitis (an inflammation or irritation of the skin).

For the most part, though, a canine is exhibiting natural, healthy behavior when it rolls on its back. So the next time your dog soils itself by going nuts in a pile of dung, don't be alarmed. Your beloved pooch is simply obeying the ancient commands of its genes.

Q Are there gay animals?

A Your heart has to go out for Bible-thumping zealots—they've had a pretty rough century, with many of their central tenets having been pummeled by the profane fists of science. No such thing as evolution? Wrong. Earth is six thousand years old? Way off. Dinosaurs never existed? Sorry. Even the last bastion of Biblical literalism—that homosexuality is unnatural—is taking a beating from the godless scientists. That's because zoologists are in wide agreement that a huge percentage of the animal kingdom exhibits homosexual behavior.

Scientists have been observing homosexual behavior in the animal kingdom for thousands of years; Aristotle first noticed hyenas behaving "unnaturally" almost twenty-three hundred years ago. But for centuries, writing about gay animals was a taboo subject among scientists. And it's no wonder, considering that most Western countries viewed homosexuality as unnatural and a crime against nature. But with the growing acceptance of homosexuality in popular culture, scientists have finally been able to come out of the closet with their secrets. And what they have revealed is fascinating.

It turns out that numerous species—more than fifteen hundred, according to some counts—exhibit the love that dare not speak its name. Interestingly, some ape species are particularly prone to homosexuality. (Fortunately, Bible-wielding folks don't believe in evolution, or they'd be troubled by the implications of this.) Meanwhile, giraffes, penguins, beetles, parrots, warthogs, fruit bats, and even right whales have been observed engaging in homosexual behavior.

There is such a massive amount of research detailing homosexuality in the animal kingdom that the University of Oslo's Natural History Museum opened an exhibit in 2006 detailing the vast array of gay animals. Though the conservative Christian movement denounced the exhibit and protesters suggested that the organizers would "burn in hell," it was a resounding success.

And here's a tidbit that might interest parents, regardless of their beliefs: When it comes time to tell your kids about the facts of life, consider that, according to researchers at the Oslo Natural History Museum, there's a relatively good chance that some birds and bees are gay.

Q Why don't penguins and polar bears get frostbite?

A If you spent an afternoon strolling around barefoot at the North Pole or the South Pole, your feet would freeze and—best-case scenario—you'd end the day short a couple of toes. But polar bears and penguins obviously don't wear boots, and they seem to be fine. What's the deal?

Scientists tell us that the human body evolved to its present state on the toasty African plains, where ice and subzero temperatures are barely imaginable. It's no surprise, then, that your body can't function without significant protection in arctic conditions. When your extremities—your feet and hands—get very cold, your body does something that may seem counterintuitive. As an act of self-preservation, it lets your extremities get *colder*, constricting the blood vessels that feed those parts in order to conserve heat for the rest of the body. This helps maintain your core temperature in frigid weather, but it wreaks havoc on your hands and feet. The eventual result is frostbite—the tissue dies off. It can also lead to hypothermia, a dangerous drop in overall body temperature, even if the rest of your body is bundled up.

Polar bears don't have this problem because their feet are like natural boots. Their huge paws come equipped with thick pads on the bottom and heavy fur on top. This thick insulation keeps their paws from losing heat rapidly, so there's no need for the bear's body to cut off the blood flow.

The furry, padded-feet approach wouldn't work so well for penguins. For one thing, they need relatively unencumbered feet so that they can swim quickly. Perhaps more importantly, since they're covered in feathers and insulated by layers of fat, their feet are their only means for releasing excess heat when they exert a lot of energy. As a result, penguins evolved highly efficient self-warming feet.

As in humans, the flow of blood to penguins' feet is controlled in order to regulate overall temperature loss. But the blood vessels in their feet are arranged differently than those of humans: The vessels that carry warm blood into the feet are located close to the vessels that take cold blood out of the feet. The warm blood heats up the cold blood that's flowing back into the torso, which prevents their overall body temperature from plummeting. What's more, their bodies are calibrated to keep their feet just a degree or two above freezing; this wards off frostbite.

Penguins have another trick to keep their feet warm. When it gets really cold, a penguin might rest on its heels and tail to keep the majority of its footpads off the ice. As for you? We recommend insulated boots.

Q Do hyenas really laugh?

A If they do, they have a really weird sense of humor. Spotted hyenas, the biggest and most aggressive of the three distinct hyena species, do indeed make noises that are reminiscent of human laughter. But they make these sounds regardless of whether anything funny is happening.

The noises, which sound more like maniacal cackles from the loony bin than chortles from *The Tonight Show* audience, seem to play an important role in the elaborate social life of the spotted hyena. These hyenas aren't solitary animals; in areas where prey is plentiful, they flourish in large clans that can include as many as a hundred members. They hunt at night in small packs that overwhelm much larger animals, such as antelope and wildebeests. The clans are highly territorial—they work together to keep other clans out of their area. And just like other social mammals (wolves, dolphins, and humans, for example), hyenas have a repertoire of noises that help them to coordinate their efforts and maintain order.

Zoologists have identified a dozen distinctive calls that hyenas mix and match to communicate a wide range of messages. It's believed that the so-called laughing noise indicates excitement and submission. For example, hyenas giggle to each other at a kill site as they divvy up the meat based on status within the clan. An equally weird, even comical noise is the spotted hyena's louder whooping call: Each hyena makes a distinctive whoop to identify itself to other hyenas and call for their support.

So if you come across a bunch of giggling hyenas while strolling through sub-Saharan Africa, don't be offended. They're not laughing at your safari outfit—they just want some of your delicious wildebeest sandwich. Or, perhaps, a piece of you.

Q Do dogs have belly buttons?

A Well, yes, in a way. A dog, like most mammals, has a scar on its abdomen that represents where the "umbilicus" was attached. The umbilicus is the cord that links the growing animal to the placenta in its mother's womb and provides the nutrients that are necessary for development. Dogs, cats, cows, sheep—all of these mammals have a "belly button," except that it's not really a "button." Instead, it's just that faint scar. On your pooch, it'll be a little hairless line below the ribcage.

Now, you may be wondering why a human, the most highly evolved mammal, has such a crude-looking belly button? It's a function of how we're born. In order to survive birth itself—being forced through the narrow birth canal—humans are born less developed and more malleable than many mammals. Thus, the umbilical cord is thicker and quite "alive" in a human birth. In many other mammals, the umbilical cord is less important toward the end of the pregnancy, so it already has begun to atrophy when the offspring is born.

We're "placental," meaning that our nourishment comes from the placental sac that's in our mother's womb. There are nearly four thousand placental mammals, ranging from rodents to bats.

Other mammals receive prenatal nourishment somewhat differently. Marsupials, such as the kangaroo, develop by sucking on a teat in a pouch on their mother's body. And monotremes, such as the platypus, are born from mammalian eggs. These, and even birds, spend some of their prenatal lives attached to a source of nutrition, but strictly speaking, only placental-type mammals develop by means of umbilical cords and, therefore, have belly buttons.

And of all those placental-type mammals, humans are exclusive in one key regard: the use of plastic surgery to make the belly button more "attractive."

Q Why does a rattlesnake's tail rattle?

A People have ascribed many functions to the rattlesnake's rattle: attracting a mate, hypnotizing prey, calling other rattlers to arms. But because a rattler rarely rattles if the snake isn't startled or perturbed, the consensus seems to be that the main purpose of the feature is to warn nearby animals to keep their distances—all those except potential meals, that is.

The distinctive rattle was especially useful in the days of yore, when rattlesnakes were contending with thundering herds of big, hoofed bison on the American plains. It was beneficial for all concerned: The snake avoided getting trampled, and the other guy avoided a venomous bite.

A rattlesnake's rattle is made of keratin, the same hard stuff that's in fingernails and animal horns. Rattlesnakes are hatched with a "pre-button," a sort of starter rattle at the end of the tail. Soon, a larger keratin rattle segment, called a button, grows at the end of the tail, beneath the skin. When the snake sheds its skin for the first time—about ten days after emerging from the egg—it sheds the pre-button, but not the button.

The button forms the first real rattle segment, while a new keratin segment starts forming at the end of the tail, behind the button. When the snake sheds its skin again, the new segment pushes the button farther out, and another segment starts forming at the base of the tail. The process repeats itself each time the snake sheds its skin—typically, three to four times a year—and a new rattle segment is added. Basically, the tip of the tail is a segment-producing assembly line.

The segments grow in puzzle-piece shapes—this keeps them loosely attached. And this is why the rattle rattles: The segments have enough flexibility to click and clack together when the snake shakes its tail. To sound the alarm, the snake sticks its tail straight up and shakes it; the tail can move back and forth ninety times per second. The click-clack is so effective that some other varieties of snakes that have rattle-envy do lo-fi versions by rapidly shaking their tails in dried leaves.

These imitators obviously know that the rattle serves an important purpose. It's kind of like a sign that reads: KEEP MOVING, BUDDY, THERE'S NOTHING TO SEE HERE.

Q Do birds of prey really fly off with small dogs?

A Unless it's an escapee from Jurassic Park, you don't have to worry about a flying predator swooping in and snatching your English bulldog or German shepherd. But if your dog can fit into a purse, there's a chance it can fit into a pair of talons.

Hawks and owls live in most parts of the United States and like to feast on small mammals such as rabbits and skunks. These creatures are similar in size to many dogs recognized as a "toy" breed by the American Kennel Club.

Most hawks and owls aren't large enough to lift an animal that weighs more than five pounds. But the smaller the dog, the greater the risk. Small dogs are inviting targets for migrating birds, which are always on the lookout for a quick meal. On the bright side, some dogs that are picked up are dropped when the bird tires and is unable to carry the weight.

Tethering a dog outside or confining it in a closed area can keep it from wandering off, but it also makes it more susceptible to a hungry predator from above. The 2008 disappearance of a dog from the fenced-in yard of a Florida doggy daycare business was blamed on nearby hawks. The center responded by adding a mesh covering.

The best way to keep a small dog safe from flying predators is to accompany it outdoors or make certain it's in the company of larger animals. Nevertheless, these precautionary measures don't always do the trick.

Here's a somewhat disconcerting example: In 2006, an eleven-year-old Boston boy took his dachshund, Dimi, outside on a leash and quickly found himself fighting off a red-tailed hawk that was attacking the puppy. "I felt a tug, and I look back and a hawk was on the back of my dog, trying to eat him," said the sixth-grader. But this story has a happy ending: He gave the bird several swift kicks and won the battle over little Dimi.

Q Are there real sea animals that are made of glass?

A If you visit Harvard University's Museum of Natural History, you can view a small gallery that is filled with glass sea creatures that are so life-like, they look as if they were just pulled from an aquarium. Of course, they're not really alive. They are the work of Leopold and Rudolf Baschka, nineteenth-century artists who specialized in creating scientific models.

But if you drop by Dr. Joanna Aizenberg's Biomineralization and Biometrics Lab in the nearby Harvard School of Engineering and Applied Sciences, she will tell you that there are indeed real sea creatures that are made of glass. She has spent her career studying *euplectella aspergillum,* a sea sponge commonly known as Venus's flower-basket. This simple but intriguing organism weaves its lacy exoskeleton from naturally generated glass.

Silicon dioxide (a.k.a. silica), a chemical compound found in quartz and sand, is the main ingredient in glass that is made by humans. Seawater contains minute particles of silica, and the Venus's flower-basket siphons them into its cells and combines them with proteins to construct glass fibers that are two hundred nanometers wide, less than one-hundredth the thickness of a human hair. These tiny fibers are then glued together with additional enzymes to make rods for the flower-basket's lattice-like glass house. This smooth, hollow structure can rise nearly a foot from the ocean floor.

Unlike humans who live in glass houses, Venus's flower-basket has no need to fear stones or anything else that might be thrown its way. Its glass exoskeleton is extremely strong—a hundred times stronger than manmade glass, according to Aizenberg—and flexible. "You can bend them, twist them, and they probably won't break because the energy of the force you apply is dissipated in the glue," Aizenberg told MSNBC in 2005.

Most remarkably, the sponge makes glass without the use of heat. Human glassmaking can require temperatures of 3,100 degrees Fahrenheit or more. Venus's flower-basket can perform the same feat in tropical waters that are three hundred and fifty to a thousand feet deep, where temperatures might average fifty degrees.

The precise process the flower-basket uses to engender glass is not clear. Professor Daniel Morse—director of the University of California, Santa Barbara, collaborative technologies program—believes that unraveling the mystery might give a boost to the fiber optics industry. Morse hopes to be able to grow fiberglass semiconductors in a test tube, in much the same way that Venus's baskets grow in the ocean. He is also examining other sponges that contain glass, such as the orange puffball, a small rock-clinging organism that keeps its glass fibers hidden inside its body.

Understanding the biochemistry of these sponges could also give a boost to the production of inexpensive, high-efficiency solar-energy panels, Morse says. It's mind-blowing to think that in the twenty-first century, people might be able to heat their homes using technology that was developed in the cold and lightless ocean millions of years ago.

Q Do snakes really slither up into toilets?

A We hesitate to tell you this, since it might lead to a lifetime of bathroom paranoia, but snakes (and other nasty animals) do indeed climb up through toilets now and again. And yes, some have bitten people who have been going about their "business."

There are two ways for an animal to make its way up into your toilet. First, if your house is connected to a municipal sewer system, the drain leading from your toilet connects to a large network of pipes that go all the way to a sewer treatment plant. This network has many small entry points, including manholes and other people's toilets.

Because of the food everyone washes down the sink, these pipes are popular hangouts for rats; because there are delicious rats everywhere, the pipes also are popular with snakes. Water rarely fills the pipes all the way and usually moves slowly, so snakes and rats can come and go as they please. Every once in a while, a snake or a rat will follow a pipe all the way to a toilet, swim through the little bit of water in the bowl, and pop out to see what's going on.

The second way in is much quicker. Most houses have vents that run from the sewage drainpipes to the roof. These allow noxious sewer gas to escape without stinking up the house. If these vents aren't covered, rats, snakes, frogs, and even squirrels can fall in and land unexpectedly in the main drain line. They scurry for the nearest exit: the toilet. (It's probably a good idea to cover those vents if you haven't already.)

There have been many reported cases of unexpected toilet visitors, including a venomous water moccasin that bit a Jacksonville, Florida, woman in 2005 and a baby brush-tailed possum that crawled out of a toilet in Brisbane, Australia, in 2008. If you have a snake phobia, the creepiest story might be that of Keith, a ten-foot-long boa constrictor that kept poking out of toilets in an apartment building in Manchester, England, in 2005. The snake, a pet that its owner had set free after being evicted, lived the high life, eating sewer rats and freaking people out for months before a building resident lured him into a bucket.

Take this as a warning not to dilly-dally for too long in the bathroom. There are safer places to catch up on your reading.

Chapter Seven

HISTORY

Q Who's the idiot who named a floating hunk of ice Greenland?

A Let's face it: Explorers weren't always the brightest of the bunch. Brave? Yes. Self-reliant? Maybe. But intelligent? Not so much. To be fair, the great explorers of yore were working without reliable maps. Nevertheless, one has to admit that it was boneheaded for Christopher Columbus to think that an island in the Caribbean was India. Or what about the guy who landed on an enormous iceberg and decided to call it Greenland? Talk about a moron.

Greenland, perhaps best known as the largest island that is not a continent, sits way up in the north Atlantic near the Arctic Circle.

Ninety percent of the island is covered by an ice cap and smaller glaciers, which means that the place is mostly uninhabitable. Although the northern coasts of Greenland had been settled for thousands of years by Inuit (the same folks who brought you the igloo), the island was largely unknown to Europeans until the late tenth century.

So how did a country that boasts almost no green land get the name Greenland? Theories abound, including the legend that Iceland switched names with Greenland to avoid being invaded by barbarians. (Barbarians were dumb, but not that dumb.) While this explanation borders on preposterous, it's not as far off the mark as you may think.

Many historians believe that Greenland's name may be derived from one of the biggest—and earliest—marketing scams of all time. In the tenth century, a Viking named Erik the Red fled his home of Iceland after committing murder. Erik took the opportunity to explore the islands and lands to the west of Iceland.

Drifting across the Atlantic, Erik eventually came to the rocky coast of an enormous island that was covered in ice. He had an idea: If he couldn't be with his people, then he'd bring his people to him. Though only a sliver of land was actually green, he promptly named the island Greenland, which, according to the Icelandic sagas, was because "men will desire much the more to go there if the land has a good name."

Icelanders, believing the marketing hype, came in droves, settling along the southern coast of Greenland, where they flourished for several hundred years. To be fair to Red, archaeologists believe that the climate was a bit more temperate during the Vikings' heyday. Still, calling this arctic landmass Greenland is a bit like a modern-day housing developer grandly naming its cookie-cutter development Honey Creek, even though the only "creek" nearby is a sewage canal. At any rate, Erik the Red pulled off one heck of a real-estate swindle.

Interestingly, it was Erik the Red's son, Leif Ericsson, who is widely considered to be the first European to visit North America. In the early eleventh century, Leif ventured with a band of explorers across the Atlantic Ocean, where he discovered the cold, wintry islands of what are now Newfoundland and Labrador, Canada. Leif named his new settlement as only the son of Erik the Red could: Wine Land.

Q Did any congressmen vote against entering World War II?

A Only one—a congresswoman, actually. After Japan bombed Pearl Harbor on December 7, 1941, the American people were just about as unified as Americans get. Before the attack, the nation had been divided over whether to enter the war. But as soon as news of the bombing spread, the determination to act was overwhelming. President Franklin Delano Roosevelt delivered a rousing speech to a joint session of Congress, requesting a declaration of war. The Senate immediately voted for the resolution, 82 to 0. In the House of Representatives, 388 people voted for the resolution, forty-one did not vote, and one voted against it.

The sole dissenting voice was Jeanette Rankin, a sixty-one-year-old pacifist Republican representative from Montana. When her name was called, she said, "As a woman, I can't go to war, and I refuse to send anyone else." Her words spurred loud booing from her fellow representatives. When Germany and Italy declared war against the United States on December 11, Congress voted unanimously to go to war against the two nations. In this case, Rankin voted present instead of no.

No one should have been surprised by Rankin's original no vote, given her background. She had made history in 1917 when she became the first woman in Congress; at the time, most states hadn't even given women the right to vote. However, her political career hit rough waters almost immediately. Her first vote came just four days after she took office, when President Woodrow Wilson asked Congress to approve his declaration of war against Germany. Rankin was one of fifty representatives to vote against the resolution, but the press singled her out—many used her stance as an argument against women's suffrage. Congressional redistricting in Montana kept Rankin from running for re-election, so she ran for the Senate instead. She lost, due in part to her opposition to the war.

For the next two decades, Rankin stayed in the political arena as a lobbyist, pushing for better health care for children, among other causes. Then in 1940 she won one of Montana's congressional seats again after campaigning on an anti-war platform. But the tides shifted with Pearl Harbor, and her no vote effectively ended her career in public office. On her way back to her office after the vote, she even had to hide out in a phone booth to escape an angry mob.

Rankin stayed active in public policy over the years, however. And in 1968, at the age of 87, she led more than five thousand women, who called themselves "the Jeanette Rankin Brigade," in a march on Washington to protest the war in Vietnam. Given all of the political flip-flopping of today, you at least have to admire her consistency.

Q What did Custer stand for in his last stand?

A Gold and his own ego, mostly. Custer's Last Stand (a.k.a. the Battle of Little Bighorn) was the culmination of years of hostility between the United States government and the Sioux Indian tribe. In the 1860s, the U.S. Army battled Sioux and other tribes in the Dakota and Wyoming territories for control of the Bozeman Trail, a path that passed through Sioux buffalo-hunting grounds to gold mines in Montana. The government abandoned the effort in 1868 and negotiated the Fort Laramie Treaty, which gave the Sioux, Cheyenne, and Arapaho tribes ownership of much of what is now South Dakota.

Then in 1874, Lieutenant Colonel George Armstrong Custer led an expedition to the area to find a suitable location for an army post and investigate rumors of gold. He verified that there was gold in the Black Hills, on Indian land. The government tried to buy back the land, but renegade Sioux Indians who refused to abide by U.S. regulations blocked the sale. The government issued an ultimatum that all Sioux warriors and hunters report to reservation agency outposts by a certain date; failure to comply would be viewed as an act of hostility.

When the renegade Sioux warriors ignored the order, the army mounted a campaign to round them up and force them into designated areas on the Indian reservation. Brigadier General Alfred Terry led the campaign, and Custer commanded one of the regiments, the Seventh Cavalry. Terry ordered Custer to lead his regiment to the south of the presumed Sioux location and wait until Terry positioned the rest of the soldiers to the north; this way, they could advance simultaneously from both sides.

But on June 25, 1876, Custer came across a Sioux village in the Valley of Little Bighorn and decided to attack it by himself. Against the advice of his officers, he divided his regiment into three groups: one to scout the bluffs overlooking the valley; one to start the attack on the upper end of the village; and one—made up of 210 men, including Custer—to attack from the lower end of the village.

Bad plan. As many as three thousand Sioux and Cheyenne men (many more than Custer had expected) forced the first group of soldiers into retreat, and then they turned their full attention to Custer and his men, killing every last one in less than an hour. News reports right after the incident said that Custer's actions were the result of foolish pride. But before long, he had morphed into a heroic figure, one who fueled outrage against the Indians in the West.

Drawings and paintings depicting the battle, usually titled "Custer's Last Fight" or "Custer's Last Stand," kept the battle fresh in people's minds for decades to follow. "Stand," in the military terminology of the day, meant simply the act of opposing an enemy rather than retreating or yielding. Custer definitely stood for that, if nothing else.

Q Why would the Democrats choose an ass as their mascot?

A Those who were at a Democratic Party rally in Jefferson City, Missouri, in August 2004 might think that they know the answer to this question. That's because they would have seen John Kerry—the Democratic candidate for the highest, most dignified office in the United States—embarrass himself and his supporters by awkwardly plucking an electric guitar onstage while wearing a cowboy hat that was far too large for his narrow cranium. On that evening, anyway, the choice of an ass as the Democratic mascot seemed perfectly fitting.

Though it may be hard to believe, the jackass was the unofficial Democratic mascot long before John Kerry stood on stage in Missouri—in fact, it's been around almost as long as the party has. The Democrats-as-donkey movement began in 1828, when Republican opponents of Democratic presidential nominee Andrew Jackson labeled him a "jackass" in the press. In reality, Jackson was indeed a bit of a jackass—he was stubborn, un-educated, and savage. But in a brilliant bit of rhetorical strategy, Jackson co-opted the term, taking pride in his reputation for stub-bornness. The Democrats used the donkey on campaign posters, and the ass became associated with Old Hickory throughout his political career.

The donkey may have gone the way of the dodo, though, if not for political cartoonist Thomas Nast. In the 1870s, he began using the donkey to represent the Democratic Party, and the symbol caught on. Incidentally, Nast is also responsible for the Republican mascot, the elephant. But while the Republicans have officially adopted the elephant as their mascot, the Democrats have been slow to follow suit—though they do use it on official party paraphernalia with regularity. Their uneasiness is understandable, considering the connotations of the jackass in the popular mind.

Of course, it could be worse. The Democrats are probably grateful that Jackson chose to associate himself with a jackass, especially when you consider one of his other nicknames when he was president: Indian Killer.

Q How many Germans were actually Nazis?

A The Nazis, or National Socialist German Workers' Party, ruled Germany with an iron fist from 1933 to 1945, but they never actually achieved official majority support from the German people, either in the form of votes or party membership.

Adolf Hitler became the Nazi Party chairman in 1921, but the German government banned the party in 1923 after a failed Nazi coup attempt. Hitler reconstituted the party in 1925 and, over the course of five years, built it from a peripheral splinter group into one of the leading conservative political parties in Germany. However, it still didn't have enough support to win a majority of votes in any election. In April 1932, Hitler garnered a mere 36.8 percent of the vote in his bid to become the leader of Germany, losing out to the incumbent, Paul von Hindenburg. That same year in July, however, the Nazis received 37.8 percent of the vote in parliamentary elections, the most among Germany's parties.

The second-biggest party, the Social Democrats, was threatened by the Nazi Party's rise. In an attempt to build a coalition government between the two parties (united against the communists), Hindenburg appointed Hitler as the new chancellor (head of the government) on January 30, 1933. At that point, there were about 1.4 million card-carrying Nazi Party members, which was less than 3 percent of the German population.

The Social Democrats hoped to control Hitler more effectively by giving him nominal power. But as chancellor, Hitler got the foothold he needed to turn Germany into a totalitarian dictatorship. Hindenburg called for new parliamentary elections in March 1933, and the Nazis turned up their intimidation tactics to sway voters away from the opposition. But even after fighting dirty, the Nazis won only 43.9 percent of the vote. The following July, Hitler declared the Nazi Party the sole political party of Germany, effectively ending democratic rule.

Even under totalitarian oppression, most Germans never joined the Nazi Party. Hitler made membership mandatory for only higher-level civil servants and bureaucrats. In fact, from May 1933 to May 1939, party membership was, for the most part, closed—Hitler wanted the Nazis to include a select elite rather than the entire German population. According to the Nazi Party's official *Zentralkartei* (master file), there were 7.2 million Nazi Party members between its reconstitution in 1925 and its dissolution in May 1945, the vast majority of whom joined after Hitler came to power. Based on these numbers, only around 10 percent of Germany's citizens were card-carrying Nazis.

If you define Nazis more broadly, as people who believed in the party's cause, it's impossible to determine the actual number. After Germany's crushing defeat in World War II, people weren't exactly clamoring to confess their past Nazi loyalties.

Q Were the Viking berserkers really berserk?

A Depending on whom you ask, the Viking berserkers were either bloodthirsty thugs intent on pillaging everything in their path or an elite corps of buff warriors who had a hard time keeping their shirts on in the heat of battle.

The word "berserk" comes from Old Norse. It has been translated as "bare of shirt," meaning that the berserkers entered battle without armor and possibly bare-chested, or more literally as "bear-shirt," for the Vikings also liked to don the skins of their totem animals (bears and wolves). Sometimes they would even wear animals' heads as helmets or masks, the better to frighten their enemies. Such behavior jibes with the English definition of the word: "extremely aggressive or angry."

Vikings first sailed into European history in AD 793, when a group of longboats pulled up on the northeast coast of England right outside the abbey of Lindisfarne. Locals thought the boats—with their high, carved prows—were literally sea dragons and that the men

who disembarked from them were equally possessed of supernatural powers.

After sacking Lindisfarne, the Vikings terrorized Europeans for the
better part of the next two centuries, looting cities and villages,
killing men, and seizing women and children and carting them
off as slaves. The most fearsome of these raiders called themselves the sons of Odin. According to Norway's epic poet Snorri
Sturluson, those who belonged to the cult of Odin "went to battle
without armor and acted like mad dogs or wolves. They bit into
their shields and were as strong as bears or bulls. They killed men,
but neither fire nor iron harmed them. This madness is called
berserker-fury."

How did they reach this state of madness or *berserkergang,* as
the Scandinavians say? In 1956, psychiatrist Howard Fabing
introduced the theory that the berserkers psyched themselves for
battle with bites of *Amanita muscaria,* a potent hallucinogenic
mushroom that is native to northern Europe. The notion that the
Vikings owed their victories to psychedelic highs is intriguing, but
it's unconvincing to many historians. Although the old Norsemen
often went heavy on the mead (a fermented beverage made from
honey), there's no archaeological evidence that they added mush-
rooms to their pre-battle menu.

Some scholars think that the berserkers may have been genetically
prone to manic-depressive syndrome. Contemporary accounts
depict them as swinging from states of wild rage to utter lassi-
tude, a pattern in keeping with what we know of bipolar disorder.
People in manic phases can experience huge releases of endorphins, which may explain why the berserkers seemed impervious
to pain.

Or it is possible that the berserkers simply worked themselves into frenzied states through dancing, drumming, chanting, and other high-energy rituals. Whatever they did, it was certainly effective: The image of the Viking warrior has hardly dimmed through the ages, though their press has gotten slightly better. Today film-makers are more apt to depict the berserker as a brave hero rather than a rapacious villain. And, of course, there are those fanatics in Minnesota who paint their faces purple just to watch football games. Now that's really berserk.

Q What did cowgirls do in the Old West?

A Here's one thing they didn't do: spend a lot of time chatting with biographers. Although it's generally acknowledged that there were plenty of women whose work was indispensable on the ranches of the American frontier—just like their more glorified male counterparts—their travails are not well documented. It wasn't until the late nineteenth century that cowgirls came into their own, and by then the Old West was fading into history.

The cowgirls who achieved their fame in the 1890s did just about everything that the cowboys of the day did: They competed and performed in public, demonstrating their riding, roping, and trick shooting skills. And that's it. Gone were the days of driving herds across the dusty plains; cowboys and cowgirls had become rough-and-tumble entertainers. True cow-folk were a thing of the past.

The genuine cowboy lifestyle flourished for only about twenty-five years, from the end of the Civil War in 1865 until around 1890.

This is when cattle ranching on the Western frontier was extremely lucrative—it's when small groups of men rounded up herds, watched over them in the open country, and drove them hundreds of miles to railroads so that they could be shipped to cities for butchering. But it didn't last. Farms took over the range; barbed wire fences enclosed the herds; and ranches were built close to railroads. Consequently, long drives became unnecessary.

Even as the lifestyle was disappearing, the Old West was being romanticized and cowboys were becoming larger-than-life heroes. Their independence and freedom inspired a nation that felt more and more constrained by city life and industrial drudgery. Wild West shows like Buffalo Bill Cody's began to appear—they were hugely popular events in which large casts of performers entertained crowds with trick riding, roping, and other cowboy feats that evoked the rugged freedom of the plains.

And this is where cowgirls first appeared. Although women had carried much of the burden of ranch work in the Old West, they weren't doing the glamorized jobs of the cowboys. But once cowboys became entertainers rather than laborers, talented women could join in the fun.

The most famous cowgirl of her day was Lucille Mulhall. Born in 1885, Mulhall honed her skills while growing up on her family's ranch in Oklahoma. On her way to becoming the women's world champion in roping and tying wild steers, she appeared frequently in her father's Wild West show and was, for a time, the featured performer from an all-star cast in the Miller Brothers' 101 Ranch Real Wild West Show. Will Rogers dubbed her the "world's first cowgirl," which probably came as news to women like Annie Oakley, who had been performing in Wild West shows for years.

Then there was Fannie Sperry Steele, who was born in 1887 in Montana. Steele was a world champion bronc rider and could also handle firearms with aplomb. After establishing herself as a rodeo star, she and her husband put together their own touring Wild West show. Steele remained active past age seventy, running a guest ranch in Montana.

Steele lived long enough to see herself become immortalized. In 1978, she was inducted into the National Cowgirl Museum and Hall of Fame in Fort Worth, Texas, where what little history there is of cowgirls is lovingly collected and preserved.

Q Who was Montezuma, and why did he want revenge?

A As Fred Willard's character puts it in the movie *Waiting for Guffman,* "Montezuma's revenge is nothing more than good old-fashioned American diarrhea. Adult diapers should never enter the picture." More specifically, it's a general term for the diarrhea that afflicts about half of the tourists who visit Mexico and Central America, and it's caused by contaminated food and water. While the locals aren't totally immune, they have generally built up a better resistance to the disease-carrying microbes that are responsible for the runs.

The nickname, which became popular in the 1960s, refers to Montezuma II, a sixteenth-century Aztec emperor. From 1502 to 1520, Montezuma ruled the Aztec Empire in what is now southern Mexico, greatly expanding its reach and wealth by conquering other indigenous tribes. Everything was going swimmingly for Montezuma until the Spanish conquistador Hernán Cortés and his men showed up in 1519. According to some accounts, Montezuma and others believed that the Spaniards were gods whose coming was foretold by prophecy. But the Spaniards may have started this legend themselves after the fact. In any event, Montezuma welcomed Cortés and his men as honored guests and showered them with gifts.

Before long, Cortés had set his sights on claiming the Aztec land and the civilization's considerable gold for Spain. His first step was to capture Montezuma and hold him as a sort of hostage. By threatening Montezuma, Cortés attempted to subdue the Aztecs and persuade them not to resist the Spanish.

But many in the Aztec capital resented the Spanish and began to look down on Montezuma. When the Aztec people revolted against the conquistadors, Cortés commanded Montezuma to address the crowd and convince them to submit. Instead, they pelted Montezuma with stones. The emperor died three days later, though it's not clear whether his injuries were to blame or whether the Spanish executed him.

The revolt pushed the Spanish out of the capital, and eventually a new leader, Cuauhtemoc, took control to lead the resistance against Cortés. In the spring of 1521, the Spanish laid siege to the capital city; Cuauhtemoc and his people surrendered after several months. In just a few years, Cortés brought the Aztec Empire to an end.

So if the spirit of Montezuma is still lurking in Mexico, it makes sense that it might exact vengeance on foreign visitors. But if you're ever in Mexico, it's best not to joke about Montezuma's revenge. Jimmy Carter made that mistake on an official visit in 1979, sparking a minor international incident that hurt already strained relations with Mexican President José López Portillo. President Carter didn't mean anything by the comment, but the reaction was understandable. What nation wants to be known for inducing mass diarrhea?

Q Was tying someone to the railroad tracks ever a popular method of killing?

A Everybody is familiar with the scene: the hero, tied to the railroad tracks, struggling desperately as the locomotive charges onward and blows its horn loudly and futilely. Will the train stop in time? Will the hero free himself in time? He will, of course. (Sorry if we wrecked the suspense.)

More interesting, however, is the question of whether this was ever a common occurrence in real life. The scenario is perfect for a melodrama, but come on—aren't there more efficient ways of killing people?

The whole tied-to-the-railroad-tracks cliché has been around for a long time—about as long as railroads themselves. The new means of transportation, coupled with the public's insatiable hunger for unlikely melodrama, prompted a number of playwrights and hack serial writers to use the idea in the latter half of the nineteenth century. By 1913 the set-up had become such a cliché that it was lampooned in one of the first Hollywood parodies, the silent film *Barney Oldfield's Race for a Life*. Of course, for those of us who weren't alive in 1913, it was Snidely Whiplash of the Dudley Do-Right cartoons who ingrained in our prepubescent minds the idea that tying somebody to the railroad tracks was a preferred method of murder.

As it turns out, tying folks to the railroad tracks didn't just happen in Hollywood or cartoons. There are some documented cases of this dastardly occurrence happening in real-life America. Way back in 1874, for example, a Frenchman named August Gardner was abducted and robbed by three men in Indiana who pro-ceeded to tie him to the railroad tracks and leave him for dead. Gardner wrestled with his bonds as the train approached, freeing one hand and then another. As the train drew closer, he loosed one of his feet. It seemed, in classic melodramatic fashion, that our hero was going to escape with his life.

But alas, he fumbled untying the last knot—the train ran over his foot and cut it off. The plucky Gardner spent the night in a culvert, then hobbled on one foot into a nearby town, where he was able to relay his story before dying.

Of course, the number of documented cases of evil-doers tying people to railroad tracks is far smaller than silent films and Dudley Do-Right cartoons would have you believe. But that's okay—we can accept that the real world doesn't always mirror what happens in the movies or on television. Just don't try to tell us that bad guys don't really twirl their handlebar mustaches as they prepare to enact their devious plans.

Q Why are there so many outdated laws?

A There aren't as many as you might think. If you look on the Web or in books, you can find plenty of weird state and local laws—like a Kentucky statute that says you can't carry an ice cream cone in your back pocket—but many are fabricated, greatly exaggerated, or no longer on the books (notice that you never see sources or specific statute numbers listed). We couldn't find anything about ice cream cones in Kentucky's official list of statutes, for example.

Nevertheless, there are a lot of irrelevant laws out there, even if they're not as funny as Kentucky's ludicrous ice cream statute. The reasons behind many of these laws have been lost to history, but when they were created, they must have mattered to some people. A group of concerned citizens called for a halt to a particular behavior—it wanted a moral code to be enforced, and it pushed its legislature to act. And legislatures, of course, write laws. The early twentieth century was an especially fertile time for peculiar laws, as judicial opinion began to favor a legal code of highly specific statutes rather than the old system known as common law, which relied on judges to decide odd cases based on previous rulings.

Many of these peculiar laws are still around. Repealing or amending laws requires the same sort of work as enacting them—a legislature has to bring an issue before the floor and vote on it. And as anyone who has ever seen a legislature in action can attest, it takes significant time and energy for politicians to do just about anything. If an old law is silly but no one is complaining about it, a legislature will probably just ignore it.

Outdated laws aren't always irrelevant, though. Sometimes laws that are arguably outdated stay on the books precisely because they still matter to people. For example, federal law prohibits the use of a computer service to transport "any obscene, lewd, lascivious, or filthy book, pamphlet, picture, motion-picture film, paper, letter, writing, print, or other matter of indecent character" across state lines—in other words, looking at porn online is probably illegal. But the United States government and most U.S. citizens agree that it's fruitless to go after everyone who's ever peeked at Internet porn. The country would grind to a halt.

With the exception of child pornography and other clearly harmful cases, the government looks the other way when we're looking at those sleazy Web sites. And even though only a handful of people would prefer more rigorous enforcement of the law, you would be hard-pressed to find a politician who would stick his neck out by calling for a revision of it. Such an action would stir up a hornet's nest. State "blue laws" regarding drinking and other sins fall into the same category—what's outdated to one person is sacred to another.

Q Who made Greenwich, England, the world's official timekeeper?

A Cosmopolitan globetrotters—such as the editors of the F.Y.I. books—are always complaining that they never know the time in whatever city they've jetted to for lunch that day. It's understandable: Time zones *are* a little bewildering. But it could be worse—and before 1884, it was. That's the year an international committee established the world's modern time zones. For some reason, though, it opted to make Greenwich, England, the system's starting point.

Timekeeping hasn't always been as precise as it is today. For much of human history, time was largely a matter of estimation based on the position of the sun. But over the centuries, more accurate timepieces were developed; by the nineteenth century, clocks were keeping accurate time to within a fraction of a second. This was great, except that nobody could agree on what time to set the clocks to. Time was local-centric rather than universal—folks set their clocks based on the position of the sun over their particular locales, leading to slightly different times in different parts of the country. Travelers, then, had to adjust their timepieces whenever they reached a new destination.

The rise of the railway system in the nineteenth century increasingly exposed this problem. With every city keeping its own time, railroad companies were incapable of maintaining any semblance of a schedule, leading to utter havoc in rail travel: Passengers missed trains or connections because their watches were set to different times than those of the railways. Nineteenth-century train stations were confused messes that resembled O'Hare International Airport.

It became clear that something needed to be done. By the 1850s England's railways had standardized their times to London time, while France had standardized theirs to Rouen time. It was slightly more complicated in the United States, due to the nation's enormous size. But on November 18, 1883, the four time zones we Americans know and love went into effect, having been established earlier in the year by an association of railway operators that was called the General Time Convention.

This, however, didn't solve the problem of synchronizing global time. Consequently, the United States organized the International Meridian Conference in 1884, with the stated goal of selecting a global prime meridian and developing a standard "universal day." Delegates from more than two dozen countries attended the conference in Washington, D.C., and agreed that the line of longitude would pass through Greenwich, England, as the prime meridian (longitude of zero degrees) and, thus, the starting point for world time.

Why Greenwich? For hundreds of years, Greenwich had been home to the Royal Observatory; its clock was the one London used to officially set its time. By the mid-eighteen hundreds, all of the railways in England had set their timetables by Greenwich Mean Time; even before the aforementioned conference, time in England essentially had been standardized. After all, the sun had not yet set on the British Empire, and its enormous amount of international shipping was based on British-designed sea charts and schedules—charts that used Greenwich Mean Time as their foundation. For the rest of the world, it made sense to use a system that was already largely in place.

Now that we've cleared up the time zones, we've got another question: Who do we blame for Daylight Saving Time?

Q What does the "D" stand for in D-day?

A D-day—June 6, 1944, the day that Allied forces began their invasion of northwest Europe in World War II—was an extraordinary moment, to say the least. In one of the largest and most dangerous assaults in military history, the Allies stormed the beaches of Normandy, France—it is generally regarded as the most significant operation in the war.

There are many possible dramatic d-words that describe the day: doom, deliverance, death. But *the* "D" comes from (drum roll, please)...the word "day." D-day is a generic military term that means, in the words of the U.S. Department of Defense *Dictionary of Military and Associated Terms,* "the unnamed day on which a particular operation commences or is to commence." The term came into use during World War I as a way of referring to the day of a military operation before a specific date was set. In planning an operation, the military uses D-day as a time reference. For example, D – 3 means three days before D-day; D + 1 means the day after D-day.

A related term is H-hour, the actual hour the operation will begin. In the case of an amphibious assault, that would be the time the first soldiers land. The exact time line for a D-day is described in reference to H-hour. For example, at Omaha Beach (the code name for one of the main landing points of the Allied invasion at Normandy), the planned timeline called for tanks and trucks to move inland at H + 120 minutes, or two hours after the assault on the beaches began.

The "D," then, in D-day is fairly mundane—it hardly seems befitting of one of the most monumental days in American history.

Chapter Eight

BODY SCIENCE

Q Do we need our pinkie finger?

A The poor, misunderstood pinkie finger. It's the runt of the hand's five-member litter, seemingly enfeebled and insignificant. It doesn't have the varied skill set of the index finger, the power and force of the thumb, the cultural cachet of the ring finger, or the elegant expressiveness of the middle finger.

No, at first blush, the pinkie finger exists for little more than to get smashed in car doors and to occasionally probe the nostrils or ear canals. Furthermore, when you consider the activities in which we Americans are most thoroughly engaged—things like clicking remote controls, grabbing handfuls of Fritos, and hoisting industrial-size jugs of cola to our lips—it becomes even more questionable whether the pinkie is needed. After all, one of our greatest Americans, Homer Simpson, doesn't have one.

But despite the pinkie's shortcomings, biomechanics experts will tell you that our little fingers are a lot more useful than you might imagine. In fact, some doctors contend that the pinkie finger is one of the most important digits of the hand—even more important, in some cases, than the almighty index finger.

According to Dr. Nader Paksima, one of the country's leading hand specialists, the pinkie plays a critical role in maintaining a strong grip. Try it yourself: Pick up the object closest to you and try to squeeze it without the aid of your pinkie. Not easy, is it? Now try it without your index finger—no problem.

That's why people who undertake daily tasks that require a strong grip (manual laborers, for example) would be better off losing the index finger than the sweet little pinkie. Even more interesting, the middle finger will actually compensate for the loss of an index finger, so that the major tasks that the average person uses the index finger for—writing, typing, cracking open a wide-mouth brew—can still be accomplished relatively easily with the surrounding fingers.

Even if our pinkies weren't so useful, they'd have an important place in our culture. Everybody knows that a promise means absolutely nothing without the accompanying "pinkie swear." In Texas, the pinkie is needed to make the "hook 'em horns" sign. For Italian men, there would be nowhere to wear rings without pinkies. And although most Americans might be able to get by without their pinkies, it's obvious that the same can't be said for our British friends across the pond—how else would they drink their tea?

Q Why does garlic give you bad breath?

A In Gothic fiction, garlic is powerful enough to scare off vampire princes. In real life, a spicy dinner at Angelo's Ristorante may simply scare off your girlfriend. What makes garlic breath so off-putting?

Garlic, a bulbous perennial plant of the Lily family, is made up of many sulfur-containing compounds. In addition to being responsible for garlic's strong odor, these sulfurous compounds get the blame for the rotten-egg stench of well water and the wholly undeniable funk created by the skunk. At any rate, when you eat garlic, the bacteria that live in your mouth feed on these compounds and proceed to release gases that are filled with their foul fetor. The result? Holy halitosis!

But that's just the half of it. There are really two kinds of garlic breath: primary garlic breath (which strikes right after you munch on a clove) and secondary garlic breath (a relentless, lingering miasma that manifests as the sulfurous compounds in the garlic slowly metabolize and work their way through your bloodstream and get expelled through your lungs).

Says Luke LaBorde, a professor of food science at Penn State University, "The volatile garlic compounds diffuse from the blood to the air deep within the lungs, and we breathe them out." But you know what? It's not only your breath that stinks. Eat enough garlic and those blood-circulating sulfurous compounds will also start to emanate straight from your skin. And they're not Chanel No. 5.

However stinky, garlic does have some redeeming qualities. It is one of the oldest-known medicinal plants, and recent studies suggest that the sulfur-containing compounds that cause bad breath may also work to relax blood vessels, lower blood pressure, and reduce the risk of heart attack. There's even some evidence that garlic may help protect against cancer and fight off the common cold.

Want to reap the benefits of garlic without putting someone's nose out of joint? After eating it, you should brush, floss, gargle with mouthwash, or chomp on some fresh parsley, fennel, or cardamom seeds. And if you're out on a date, just make sure your significant other eats the same garlicky fare as you; simultaneous garlic breath seems to cancel out the otherwise objectionable effects. "You probably don't notice the smell because your olfactory system is saturated and your brain no longer receives 'garlic signals,'" says LaBorde. "It's the same as if you worked in a horse barn: After a while you don't notice the smell."

Q Would a hermaphrodite be sentenced to a men's or women's prison?

A It could go either way. First there was the tempest in Colorado Springs, Colorado, over Storme Aerison, who made national news in 1990 as a seventeen-year-old cheerleader at

Coronado High School. Aerison was newsworthy because she was actually twenty-six-year-old Charles Daugherty, a hermaphrodite (or intersexual) who had been raised as a boy despite having male and female sex organs. He was outed when other cheerleaders from the school noticed razor stubble poking out from under his makeup.

Some years later, after fully embracing her (his?) female side and changing her name, Aerison was charged with fraud for concocting a scam in which she claimed to be a supermodel producing a swimsuit calendar. The criminal justice system didn't know what to make of Aerison. Her inmate profile was marked with an "M" in the gender category, but court documents referred to her as "she." While awaiting trial, Aerison was held in isolation in the county jail's male ward.

Then there's the case of Miki Ann Dimarco, a Wyoming intersexual who lived as a woman and had been undergoing hormone therapy. She was sentenced in 2000 to fourteen months in the Wyoming Women's Center for violating parole on check-fraud charges, but when she arrived and underwent a strip search, officers discovered that she also had male genitalia.

The perplexed prison officials decided to place Dimarco in what was essentially solitary confinement for the duration of her sentence. Dimarco later filed a couple of lawsuits against the state that ultimately failed. (We only mention them because it gives us a chance to note that the attorney general who defended the state in the cases was named Pat Crank.)

In 2004, British hermaphrodite Jonathon Featherstone had the good fortune of getting nailed for drug smuggling in Jamaica, where prison officials were forced to admit that they had no provisions for housing an inmate of indeterminate gender. Featherstone got off relatively easy, with a suspended six-month sentence and a $4,800 fine.

Apparently, nothing confuses the penal system like a woman with a penile system.

Q Why do we get food cravings?

A Got a hankering for some steamed carrots and Brussels sprouts? Didn't think so. Most cravings are of the sweet, salty-crunchy, super-high-fat varieties. But just what is it that prompts us to make a mad dash to the 7-Eleven for Funyuns and Ding Dongs in the middle of the night?

Researchers aren't exactly sure, but one theory that's gaining acceptance speculates that food cravings are actually addictions. How so? Brain image studies conducted by Marcia Pelchat, a sensory psychologist at the Monell Chemical Senses Center in Philadelphia, show that food cravings activate parts of the brain that are typically involved with habit formation. Known as the caudate nucleus, this is the same region of the brain that's affected by cocaine, alcohol, and cigarettes. "Think of food cravings as a sensory memory," says Pelchat. "You remember how good it felt the last time you had that food."

It all has to do with a particular food's biological and emotional resonance. Brian Wansink, a food psychology expert and the author of *Mindless Eating: Why We Eat More Than We Think,* agrees that people tend to crave foods that connect them to pleasant experiences.

Men, he says, are drawn toward hearty meals—such as barbecue ribs, burgers, meatloaf, pasta, pizza—because they associate those foods with a nurturing wife or mother. Women, on the other hand, connect those same savory meals to long hours spent in the kitchen. Wansink notes that chocolate and ice cream don't involve any prep work or cleanup, which may help to explain why women are drawn to those types of sweets. That's right, ladies—just flip the lid off that pint of Häagen-Dazs, and you've got one quick euphoria fix.

But what about the "wisdom of the body" theory, which states that our bodies simply crave what we nutritionally need? Pelchat says that wisdom doesn't apply, unless you're a sodium-deficient rodent: "When rats are salt deprived, they show a sodium appetite; they seem to be able to detect amino acids when they're protein deprived. But there's actually very little evidence for that in people. A lot of people in our society crave salty foods, but very few are actually salt deficient."

So that sudden urge to hit the A&W drive-thru isn't exactly motivated by nutritional necessity. You're really just addicted to the chili cheese fries.

Q Do identical twins have a psychic connection?

A We've all heard stories about mysterious psychic connections between identical twins. Frankly, most of them sound like hogwash—fodder for M. Night Shyamalan movies. Is there any scientific proof that such a phenomenon exists?

In 2004 the National Geographic Channel tried to find out by enlisting the help of Richard and Damien Powles, nine-year-old twins from Great Britain. Their mom insisted that they had been sending signals to each other since they were a few days old. While the video cameras rolled, Richard was attached to a polygraph machine in an attic room and was wearing headphones in order to muffle any sounds. Two flights below in the living room, Damien drew pictures of Richard to focus his mind.

Over the next few minutes, Damien was subjected to a series of harmless but startling events: a balloon exploded behind him, a plate shattered, his hand was plunged into a bowl of icy water. In each instance, the polygraph measured sharp increases in his brother's breathing, heartbeat, and blood pressure, though Richard could neither see nor hear Damien. The test was later repeated in a London studio with similar results.

Was Richard sensing Damien's surprise? Possibly. But the producers of the video remained unconvinced. The experiment hadn't exactly been conducted under laboratory conditions, and a few blips on a polygraph printout could be interpreted many ways.

Randy and Jason Sklar, identical twins in their early thirties, told the magazine *Psychology Today* that they had participated in a similar test when they were fourteen. Jason was asked to draw a shape on which Randy, who was in a separate room, concentrated. No dice. "I was so far off," Jason recalled, "they ended up stopping the study." Randy and Jason are aspiring comedians, so their assessment is tinged with comic exaggeration.

But Eileen Pearlman is a stone-cold-sober PhD and a child therapist—as well as an identical twin—and she agrees with the Sklars. "There has been no scientific evidence to support ESP in twins," she told an interviewer from WebMD. She says that empathy, not telepathy, is the most likely explanation for the mental connections that many twins feel.

Nevertheless, reports of psychic twins are hard to shake off. The Rhine Research Center and Institute of Parapsychology at Duke University has been investigating twin telepathy since the early 1940s. It still hasn't demonstrated that psychic connections exist, but it hasn't proved otherwise, either.

Guy Lyon Playfair, author of *Twin Telepathy: The Psychic Connection,* is convinced something is there. His book contains a trove of intriguing anecdotes: a healthy man who collapsed at the moment his twin had a heart attack; a little girl who developed a blister on her hand in exactly the same spot where her twin's hand was burned; a woman who doubled over the instant her far-away twin went into labor. Solid evidence or compelling entertainment? Even twins themselves don't know for sure.

Meanwhile, Steve Bauman, the current head of the Rhine Center's twin telepathy study, sometimes seeks volunteers. So if you're two of a kind, you might want to give him a call. Either him or M. Night Shyamalan.

Q Is it possible to kiss your own butt?

A If you've ever been cornered at a party by a chatty, self-satisfied convert to the practice of yoga, you know that there are people who *aspire* to kiss their own butts. But is it physically possible to do so?

The answer lies in the discomforting world of contortion. Part yoga and gymnastics, part circus freak show, part sexual fetish, it's kind of a creepy world. It's where the relatively pleasant experience of viewing a young woman in a leotard can get weird in a hurry. One second she's standing there, all cute and perky; the next she's in an ultra back bend, her feet dancing about her ears.

Some of the world's most celebrated contortionists hail from Mongolia, where the act of bending one's body is an ancient art. Mongolians begin training as early as age five, and Mongolian circus performers are renowned for spectacular acts of contortion. But given this historic dedication to what they consider a noble calling, Mongolian contortionists are likely above public posterior-smooching.

To really get your contortionist freak on, you must turn to the Internet. (Big surprise.) There you'll find pictures and video of a lithe, blonde European who calls herself Zlata, "the Goddess of Flexibility." Don't miss the shot of a scantily clad Zlata seated in a chair before a stove, heels casually elevated behind her head as she sautés a skillet of onions. Hot!

A monthly fee gains you access to the "members" section of Zlata's Web site, where you can view the contortionist dressed in exotic lingerie. In one video, Zlata lies on her back in a shiny-red body suit, her legs spread impossibly wide. Slowly she bends her lower torso toward her head. Eventually, her rear end does appear to make contact with her face, though no actual kissing takes place. But once you've mastered the ability to view your own butt from that vantage point, the rest is academic.

Q Are growing pains real?

A Growing pains are real, but the name is misleading. The term "growing pains" describes a type of periodic discomfort that up to 40 percent of all children experience in their calves or thighs. The folksy explanation of this phenomenon is that the aches are caused by the rapid growth of the child's body and the extra strain this places on the muscles and tendons. While this idea has a certain amount of charm, it's not entirely true.

During childhood, the body does go through an incredible process of growth and development—but there's no reason to believe that this is painful. The rate at which a child grows is virtually imperceptible, and certainly not beyond the body's capacity to adapt. So what's behind these aches and pains? No one knows for sure. They're far from life threatening—they usually last for a short period of time and are easily mitigated by over-the-counter medicines like ibuprofen—so there hasn't been a lot of research into them. Nevertheless, there are several theories.

Some doctors believe that children who report growing pains are actually suffering from another mysterious condition, restless leg syndrome (an apparent disorder of the nervous system that affects leg sensation). Another possibility is that some children may have weak bones or a low tolerance for pain. But the prevailing wisdom is that growing pains are simply the results of particularly strenuous days of running, jumping, or whatever else it is that kids do when they're raising hell in the neighborhood.

In general, growing pains are a perfectly benign and normal part of being a child. It's unwise to ignore them completely—there are some serious but very rare conditions that can have similar symptoms, such as leukemia, juvenile arthritis, or structural bone disorders—but usually growing pains can be handled with an Advil or two. For parents, anyway, the real growing pains begin when the child reaches adolescence and totals the family car, steals their booze, or is brought home by the police.

Q Why is it more difficult to lose weight as you get older?

A As the years pass and the birthdays mount, we watch in horror as our sinewy bodies become blobs. Is there any way to halt this grotesque march into oblivion? Not really. The main problem is that we tend to lose muscle mass as we age—even if our caloric intake is modest, less muscle leads to a slower metabolism and a greater propensity to put on weight.

A pound of muscle burns about thirty-five to fifty calories per day; a pound of fat burns around three calories per day. Do the math, and you'll see that you're pretty much screwed: Even when we're not doing something strenuous, muscle will burn about twelve to seventeen times more calories than will body fat. In other words, with greater muscle mass, we have a much faster metabolism and can consume more calories before we start putting on weight. But if the ratio of fat to muscle tips to the blubbery side of things, the pounds add up.

After age 40, we typically lose about 1 percent of our lean muscle mass per year. Part of this is the natural result of the aging process: As we get older, the body produces less testosterone and human growth hormone, the two primary hormones that control muscle growth.

But our daily habits can also be significant factors. Think about it: The routine of a twenty-year-old involves a lot more physical activity than that of someone who's thirty or older. Compare walking across campus several times a day and then going out on the town to sitting at a desk for eight hours and then trudging home to sit on the couch and watch television. A sedentary lifestyle leads to less muscle mass.

Many people exacerbate the problem by going on extreme diets or skipping meals. If we cut too far back on calories or go, say, sixteen hours without eating, we can slow down our metabolisms. And when food intake dips too precipitously, the body switches into "starvation mode" and starts storing more calories as fat.

This "starvation mode" made sense when we were cavemen: Lean times could be a sign of even leaner times to come, and saving up energy was a necessary precaution. But in modern times, lean times can lead to a ballooning butt. Intense dieting actually makes weight loss more difficult to sustain because the body adapts to a lack of food and burns fewer calories.

A balanced approach is your best bet. Consume a doctor-recommended number of calories throughout the day and expend energy through cardiovascular exercise and strength training. If you build up enough muscle mass, you can boost your metabolism, push back Father Time a bit, and reclaim some of the glory of your college years. You may even be able to go streaking to the quad without breaking a sweat.

Q Can you walk on hot coals without burning your feet?

A There was a time when the feat (pun most certainly intended) of walking on hot coals was the domain of mystical yogis who dedicated their lives to pushing the physical limits of the body by using the awesome power of the mind.

Then along came reality television. Now on any given night, we can tune in to some pudgy actuary from Des Moines waltzing across a bed of glowing embers for the nation's amusement, seemingly unharmed. So what's the deal? Is walking on hot coals dangerous, or even difficult?

At the risk of prompting legions of idiots to inflict third-degree burns on themselves, the answer is no. Walking on hot coals is not as impressive as it seems—but please, please, read on before you try something stupid.

The secret to walking on hot coals has nothing to do with mental might and everything to do with the physical properties of what's involved. It comes down to how fast heat can move from one object to another. Some materials, like metal, conduct heat very well—they're good at transmitting thermal energy to whatever they touch. Think of your frying pan: You heat it up, slap a juicy steak down on it, and witness an instant sizzle—the metal easily passes its heat to an object of lower temperature. On the other hand, consider the bed of hot coals that's used for fire walks. It started out as chunks of wood—and wood is a terrible conductor of heat.

But don't go for a romp over hot coals just yet. It's also important that the hot coals are not, you know, *on fire*. If you've seen a fire-walking demonstration on TV, you may have noticed that there were no jumping flames, just smoldering embers— the coals probably had been burning for hours and had built up a layer of ash. And ash is another poor conductor of heat—sometimes it's used as insulation for this very reason.

But all the ash in the world can't help you unless you keep one final thing in mind. Think about it: What sort of gait do you see when a person is traversing a bed of hot coals? A stroll? An amble? A saunter? No, no, and no—it's all about making a mad dash. As a result, the amount of time that any one foot is in contact with a coal might be less than a second. And the exposure is not continuous, as each foot gets a millisecond break from the heat with each step.

So if you take a poor heat conductor like wood, cover it with a layer of insulation, and have intermittent exposure to the heat, the likelihood of sustaining serious burns is low. Of course, we don't advise that you try this stunt at your next backyard get-together. What if you fall? Or even slip or stumble? You'll have a lot of explaining to do at your local ER.

Q Why do you stop noticing a smell after a while?

A We should all thank our lucky stars for this phenomenon—it makes public transportation a lot more bearable, and it surely has saved countless marriages. And back in our hunter-gatherer days, it made the sense of smell a much more effective survival tool.

To understand why, we need to review the fundamentals of smelling. When you smell something, you're detecting floating molecules that were cast off from all the stuff around you. Inside your nose, you have millions of olfactory sensory neurons, each of which has eight to twenty hair-like cilia that extend into a layer of mucus. These cilia have receptors that detect molecules floating into the nose. Different receptors are sensitive to different types of molecules; for example, when a grass molecule makes its way into your nose, you don't detect it until it bumps into one of the receptors that is sensitive to that particular type of molecule. This neuron then sends a signal to a part of the brain called the olfactory bulb, which is devoted to making sense of odors.

Based on the type of receptors that have been activated, your brain tells you what kinds of molecules are wafting into your nose. You perceive this information as a unique smell. If many sensory neurons fire in response to the same type of molecule, you experience a more intense smell.

This is a handy tool in the wild because it helps you find good food, avoid bad food, and sense predators. And it works a lot better if you're able to filter out ongoing odors that are particularly pungent. For example, you would have a much harder time sniffing out delicious but distant bananas in the jungle if you were preoccupied by the pervasive smell of fetid mud. And since we animals are a naturally stinky bunch, our own body odors would drown out all kinds of useful smells if we didn't possess a means to ignore them.

It's not clear exactly how this happens, but biologists believe that it occurs at both the receptor level and inside the brain. In other words, sensory neurons in the nose reduce their sensitivities to particular types of molecules, while the brain stops paying attention to whatever indications it receives regarding those odors. This filtering process is most likely the driving force behind long-term desensitization to a smell.

It's why a factory worker might stop noticing a strong chemical smell. Or why a wife doesn't run for cover when her husband takes off his shoes after a long day.

Q Why does the belly button collect so much lint?

A It's an affliction that embarrasses most people. Some call it "dirty" and "gross"; others simply find it mysterious. When it is discussed, it's usually late at night, behind closed doors. Yes, we're referring to belly button lint. But if there's one thing we've learned in our weekly belly button lint support group, it's that this accumulation of fuzz is natural. Still, each evening as we shamefully dislodge another tuft of blue-gray lint, we wonder just where it comes from.

Fortunately for humanity, not one but two scientists have taken on the Herculean task of identifying the source and nature of belly button lint. In 2001, Australian researcher Dr. Karl Kruszelnicki embarked upon a massive survey of nearly five thousand people in order to identify the risk factors for belly button lint (BBL). What did he learn? The typical BBL sufferer is male, middle-aged, slightly paunchy, and has a hairy stomach and an "innie" navel. Kruszelnicki suggested that BBL is merely minute fibers that are shed by the clothes we wear every day. These fibers are channeled by abdominal hair into the belly button, where they collect until they are extracted. Dr. K opines that the reason most BBL is a blue-gray color is that blue jeans rub the most against the body.

Dr. Kruszelnicki's research was a landmark study in BBL, but it wasn't quite detailed enough for some people. Enter Austrian chemist Dr. Georg Steinhauser, who decided that it was necessary to spend three years of his life chemically analyzing more than five hundred samples of BBL, mostly of his own making. Along the way, Steinhauser discovered that BBL isn't merely fibers from clothes, as Kruszelnicki had believed, but also includes bits of dead skin and fat.

Steinhauser went even further, establishing a list of practices to discourage the development of BBL. Shaving the abdomen seems to be the most foolproof method, though this strategy is, of course, temporary. Wearing older clothes may also help, because they have fewer loose fibers than new duds. Additionally, a belly button ring appears to have some effect in preventing BBL.

But it's another Australian man (what is it with Aussies and belly button lint?) who has taken BBL research to a whole new level. Graham Barker has been collecting his own BBL—which he calls "navel fluff"—in jars since 1984, earning himself a spot in the *Guinness Book of World Records*. Thanks to Barker's courage, it is now safe for those afflicted with BBL to come out of the closet and show their lint-filled bellies to the world.

Q If a mother with a piercing breastfeeds her baby, will the milk come out of three holes?

A The short answer: Milk will sometimes come out of the extra holes, but it won't make any difference. Contrary to popular belief (at least among those who have never breastfed anyone), milk doesn't squirt out of a single hole in the breast even under normal circumstances.

In each nipple, a network of ducts runs from milk-producing glands called alveoli to fifteen to twenty openings, often referred to as pores. So when a woman lactates, it's not like the single stream that comes out of a baby bottle—milk seeps from the entire nipple. A piercing simply adds more holes to the equation. No big deal, right?

Of course, a woman with a piercing will want to remove the bling before breastfeeding, since the metal can carry bacteria and irritate the baby's mouth. In a worst-case scenario, the piercing could cause the baby to choke. But assuming all of the nipple rings are out, the extra holes might even aid in breastfeeding.

If you were hoping to read about spectacular breast feats—the types that are akin to Bellagio-style fountains—we're sorry to disappoint. There are no theatrics here.

Q Do old farts fart more?

A Gas. Wind. Fart. Flatus. Call it what you want, but we all do it, to the toot of about fourteen times a day. That's right—most people (even presidents and supermodels) produce one to four pints of intestinal gas daily.

However embarrassing it might be, farting is a perfectly normal process that is related to the bacterial breakdown of undigested food. Greek physician Hippocrates (considered the father of medicine) once professed: "Passing gas is necessary to well-being." And the Roman emperor Claudius even put forth an imperial decree that "all Roman citizens shall be allowed to pass gas whenever necessary."

But don't take this as permission to let one rip in the middle of your niece's piano recital. Unless you're of a certain age.

The silent but deadly truth is that as we get up in years, our gastrointestinal tracts become a bit more finicky. Our bodies produce fewer of the enzymes required to break down and absorb the sugars, starches, and fibers that are in the foods we eat. And the unfortunate results are a boatload of bloating and many barking spiders. (Spiders are, according to the *Urban Dictionary*, what "farts are blamed on when there is no dog available.")

And this particularly applies to more mature ladies. According to John A. Sunyecz, MD, president of MenopauseRx Inc., the menopause and perimenopause transition is "a peak time" for the "uncomfortable symptoms of gas and embarrassing flatulence." In fact, a national survey conducted on behalf of Beano (a natural enzyme supplement used to reduce digestive problems) found that 69 percent of women experience stomach gas during menopause. Jeez, as if the night sweats and the wild mood swings weren't trouble enough.

So what's an excessively gassy geezer (or geezeress) to do? Lay off big notorious gas-producing foods like beans, broccoli, Brussels sprouts, cauliflower, cabbage, cereals, legumes, nuts, seeds, whole grain breads, and carbonated beverages. And if that doesn't help, just pretend not to notice. Everybody knows that whoever smelt it dealt it.

Q Why does squinting help you see?

A Most of us don't think much about squinting. It's a highly underrated bodily function—it doesn't receive nearly the amount of pub that, say, belching does. But if we couldn't squint, much of the pageantry of life would elude us. (Okay, that's a bit of an overstatement, but we're trying to get a point across here.)

Light comes into your eyes as individual rays from all directions. The front of each eye has a lens that bends these rays and redirects them onto your retina, which is located at the back of the eye. This focused light forms an image on the retina, in the same way the lens on a camera bends light rays to form an image on film (or on a charge-coupled device in a digital camera).

When everything is working precisely, the lens focuses the rays directly onto the retina, forming crisp images. But for many people, the process works less than ideally. The lens bends some rays in such ways that crisp images form slightly in front of or behind the retina, not directly on it. As a result, things at certain distances appear blurry. This issue is most severe with rays that come into the eye at sharper angles (light from above or below your line of sight), because the lens bends those rays more than the ones that arrive straight on.

So how does squinting help to solve this problem? It covers the top and bottom of your eye, thereby eliminating a lot of the rays that arrive at sharp angles; your lens receives only the head-on rays. Squinting also changes the shape of your eye, in kind of the same way Lasik surgery does. All of this adds up to clearer images.

Basically, squinting acts as a filter—it blocks the peripheral information and allows only the good stuff to enter. So take a moment or two to praise this handy little visual aid. Without squinting, life would be a blurry mess. (Okay, we're exaggerating again, but you get the idea.)

Chapter Nine

SPORTS

Q Which sport is played by hookers?

A Badminton players stroke the shuttlecock. In baseball, a pitcher can't bring the heat unless he's got a rubber. A good football team knows how to use its tight end to score. And if you have a weakness for hookers, then you probably like rugby. After all, the hooker is one of the most important players on the rugby field.

Even if you know nothing about the sport, you've probably seen a scrum—that bizarre moment in a rugby match when a bunch of players get all scrunched together into a huddle and push against each other until the ball pops out. In the center of that mass of humanity is each team's hooker, shouting instructions and trying to "hook" the ball out of the scrum to waiting teammates.

On the surface, the game seems a bit absurd, but it's immensely popular. Rugby, like soccer, has a huge international following that generally doesn't include Americans. The sport's 2007 World Cup drew an estimated 4.2 billion TV viewers worldwide.

Rugby emerged in England and got its name from Rugby School, where the first official rules of the game were established in 1845. Along the way, the sport split into two versions: rugby union and rugby league. The rules and scoring differ somewhat, and a rugby union team has fifteen players while a rugby league team has thirteen. Rugby union is the more popular version these days.

To the casual American observer, rugby looks like a primitive form of football: The ball is oval-shaped, the field is rectangular (though a little larger than a football gridiron) and features goalposts, and the general idea is to advance the ball across the opponent's goal line. And indeed, football is a direct descendant of rugby, which was a relatively popular sport in North America for a brief period in the late nineteenth century and again on the West Coast in the early twentieth century (the U.S. team captured Olympic gold in 1920 and 1924).

Rugby teams also rack up their points in much the same way that football teams do. In rugby union, a try (the equivalent of a touchdown) is worth five points, a conversion (a kick through the goal posts after a try, like football's extra point) is two points, and a drop goal (which resembles a field goal) is three points. The point values differ slightly in rugby league, but the basic idea is the same.

So what separates rugby players from their American counterparts? For starters, rugby players don't wear helmets, shoulder pads, or much of any protective gear at all. (We think that they may wear athletic supporters, but we are definitely not going to ask.) The sport attracts a certain adventurous type of individual—a stout, spirited character who is full of energy and fond of malt-based beverages. For this reason, you should never make hooker jokes in the presence of rugby players. Let the F.Y.I. staff, cowering safely behind our keyboards, do that for you.

Q Why do women like men in sports uniforms?

A Ever seen Brian Urlacher's butt in HD? For the official coin toss, you could bounce a quarter right off of those tight polyester pants—and the ladies would call tails! Who says women don't like to watch sports?

The truth is, most sports uniforms are sleekly designed for freedom of movement and to prevent the opposition from grabbing onto them. But they also seem to accentuate a guy's bulging biceps, V-shaped torso, and gluteus maximus—to the max. Now, it doesn't take any kind of scientist to explain that women are more attracted to men with athletic physiques.

And isn't it kind of nice that men in sports uniforms are confident enough to wear fashionable colors—for instance, regal-gold and purple (the Los Angeles Lakers) or unconventional turquoise-teal (the Jacksonville Jaguars)? Sure beats the dingy white Hanes T-shirt with orange pit stains that your boyfriend wears every weekend.

Yep, a guy in a sports uniform just has that certain *je ne sais quoi*. Perhaps it's because unlike the skimpy bikinis in the *Sports Illustrated* swimsuit issue, men's sports uniforms leave a little something to the imagination. Ladies, wouldn't you like to know what's really going on beneath those pinstriped baseball pants and embroidered numbers? Turns out, there's a lot more happening than meets the eye.

According to evolutionary biologist Albrecht Schulte-Hostedde and sports psychologist Mark Eys of Ontario's Laurentian University, women may be unconsciously drawn to men who play team sports. Their study of 282 female undergrads ages eighteen to twenty-nine (published in the journal *Evolutionary Psychology*) found that heterosexual women prefer sexual partners who play team sports over men who play solitary sports or no sports at all. "It seems that individuals that are engaging in team sports are considered more attractive and desirable," says Schulte-Hostedde. But why?

Researchers have a few theories. One is that on a subconscious level, women believe that men on sports teams would make better parents. "You have to communicate well and be willing to take a particular role on the team," Schulte-Hostedde says. Seems that team sports allow women to gauge how well a man works with others. There are also some cultural influences at play: In North America, many team sports are considered high-status endeavors that are synonymous with wealth and power, and that always goes a long way in getting a gal's attention.

It all makes sense, doesn't it? A guy in a sports uniform looks good—and he's no slouch to boot. And you know what else? He's committed his Sunday to a whole lot more than a Barcalounger and a twelve-pack of Budweiser. Go team.

Q Is golf a sport?

A Look it up in any dictionary: "Sport" is generally defined as recreation, a competition based on skill, and a pleasurable activity. No dictionary makes any exceptions regarding the participants' bloated midsections, their lack of perspiration, or their absurd pants. You can argue until you're blue in the face, but it comes down to semantics, and golf fits the bill.

Some might argue that the frustration that accompanies four hours on the links isn't the least bit pleasurable, but how many of us would find pleasure in getting crushed by a three-hundred-pound defensive tackle? Lack of pleasure doesn't prevent us from calling football a sport, so there's no point in trying to trip up golf on this technicality.

Why not blame the inventors of this infuriating pastime instead? For years, the Scots have taken the credit. And who better to hold responsible for such a game than a bunch of miserable haggis eaters? But historical research shows that plenty of folks in many ancient cultures spent hours out in the fields pointlessly hitting balls with sticks. In the end, it looks as though the Dutch may have the closest lie. The stick in their stick-and-ball game was called a *kolf* or *kolve*.

When we're not busy trying to enforce the "he who smelt it, dealt it" code of justice, we here at F.Y.I. headquarters sometimes gaze out the window and wonder why a jittery, exhausted nineteen-year-old kid can sink a pair of game-winning free throws as fifty thousand people scream at him during the NCAA's Final Four, while a comfortable, filthy-rich, forty-something golfer demands perfect silence every time he tries to hit a ball that is sitting absolutely motionless on a tee.

Still, we can't argue with the dictionary. Golf is a sport.

Q What's the difference between karate, kung fu, and tae kwon do?

A Oh, this one is easy. Karate is the one that had its own movie, in which Arnold from *Happy Days* teaches Ralph Macchio how to wash a car while standing on one foot. Kung fu is the one that had its own TV show, in which a somewhat-Asian-looking hippie named Grasshopper roams the Old West, goading ornery, gun-slinging hombres into antagonizing him so that he can humbly murmur, "I do not wish to harm you," just before he unloads a saddlebag of hurt on them using only his hands and feet. And tae kwon do is the one that had its own radio show.

You don't remember *Tae Kwon Duo*? Every week, Dorothy Lamour and her faithful companion, Spud, patrolled the backstreets of a fictional Ohio metropolis called "Cleveland," selling War Bonds and vanquishing suspected Nazis with precisely delivered throat punches. They didn't make many episodes; the show was sponsored by the ill-fated Lucky Strikes Breakfast Cereal ("With extra nicotine for more pep!").

Okay, obviously some of that is made up. (No parents would ever really name their kid "Ralph Macchio.") But to the casual observer, karate, kung fu, and tae kwon do can be difficult to tell apart. It's all just a bunch of barefoot dudes kicking each other, right?

The three disciplines do share similarities and have surely influenced each other over the centuries; each evolved in East Asia, after all. For clarity and a bit of simplicity, we can associate each discipline with a country: karate with Japan, kung fu with China, and tae kwon do with Korea. All are mainly unarmed forms of combat (although some styles of kung fu involve weapons) that are also practiced as sport or exercise and emphasize self-defense and spiritual development.

Karate stresses timing and coordination to focus as much power as possible at the point of impact. Blows are delivered with the hands, forearms, feet, knees, and elbows. At the height of his or her powers, a karate practitioner can split boards with a swift kick or punch.

Kung fu teaches self-discipline, with all of its moves beginning from one of five basic foot positions, most of which pay tribute to animals. Traditionally, kung fu places less emphasis on levels or rankings than the other two do (indicated, for example, by the different belt colors awarded in karate).

Tae kwon do is partially based on karate and features distinctive standing and jump kicks, but punching and blocking are also integral to it, just as they are to the other two disciplines. As in karate, students of tae kwon do often spar with each other; they try to avoid injury by learning to land their kicks and punches within inches of an opponent's body.

Each discipline requires years of study to master—but, despite what you may have learned from Hollywood, none involves much use of Turtle Wax.

Q Was professional wrestling ever real?

A If it ever was, nobody's letting on now. In its current golden age, professional wrestling has learned to flaunt its spurious side, and fans are eating it up. World Wrestling Entertainment, Inc., the outfit that rules big-time pro wrestling, is a multimillion-dollar operation with shares traded on the New York Stock Exchange.

Pro wrestling was born in the humbler surroundings of the nineteenth-century carnival circuit, where strongmen would take on local challengers who paid for the chance to get into the ring and fight for prize money. The matches were fixed—sometimes with the help of the challengers and sometimes not. In any event, crowds loved the drama, and it wasn't long before the promoters realized that the challengers' entry fees were peanuts compared to the money that could be made by charging admission for folks to watch the matches.

During several peaks in wrestling's popularity—such as the 1930s, 1950s, and 1980s—everyone involved swore that the fighting was real. Wrestlers adhered to a code called "kayfabe," which is an old carnival term that means, essentially, "fake." If a wrestler stepped out of character, flouted the script, or otherwise undermined the illusion that the events were real, he was breaking kayfabe. And anybody who broke kayfabe in wrestling was not long for the sport.

This is not to suggest that wrestlers aren't athletes. A pro wrestling match is like a dangerous, brute-force ballet, and the performers have to be in excellent shape to pull off all of their moves. Pro wrestling has even gone through its own steroids scandal, just like other sports.

As for the nagging "real" thing, that's not even a question anymore. In its high-finance, twenty-first-century incarnation, professional wrestling has openly embraced the notion that the matches aren't truly competitive but are, in fact, staged according to preplanned storylines. Think of these matches as soap operas with knee drops.

Q Why is soccer popular everywhere except the United States?

A Every four years, there's a sporting event that transfixes almost the entire globe. In hundreds of countries, parades are held, commerce and transportation slow to a crawl, and the home team's chances are the topic of nearly every discussion. No, it's not the Olympics—it's the World Cup. Never heard of it? Don't feel bad—neither have many of your fellow Americans. And those who have heard of it simply don't care.

Even though playing youth soccer is a veritable rite of passage in the United States, it seems that most Americans lose interest in the sport somewhere around age twelve. It's not as if adult soccer doesn't exist in this country—there's even a professional soccer league, known as Major League Soccer, which enjoys a degree of popularity and respect that's on a level with the Professional Miniature Golf Association. Yet in the rest of the world, soccer inspires passion and rabidity. The United States' indifference to soccer has baffled sports journalists and analysts for decades. Here are a few theories:

- **We don't like games in which you can't use your hands.** Some observers have pointed out that the myth of America is largely constructed upon the idea of the self-made, hardworking man. A man who uses his hands to build houses with hand-cut logs and hand-laid bricks, who uses his hands to plow the earth and bake his bread. That none of this has happened for a hundred and fifty years makes little difference to this theory's proponents.

- **We don't like games without action or scoring.** Soccer seems pretty boring, especially to the uninitiated. A lot of kicking the ball across a field, with very little effort being made to advance to the other team's goal. Games often end in ties or with a total tally of fewer than three goals. Yes, watching soccer for a few hours can be pretty deadening.

- **We don't like prissy athletes.** Have you ever watched a soccer game? Two-thirds of it consists of players flopping lamely or gesticulating wildly when they get called for a penalty. We

Americans are stand-up guys, always behaving courteously, willing to take the blame when it's our fault and the first to admit we're wrong when we're wrong. Okay, maybe not so much—as evidenced by the steroids scandal in baseball.

The most likely reason Americans don't like soccer is that, quite frankly, we suck at it. America has a big ego, and getting crushed in soccer by countries like Colombia and Costa Rica doesn't do much to inflate it.

The problem, though, is that if we don't pay attention to the sport, we'll probably never field a team that's good enough to be consistently competitive on the international stage. This will further suppress national interest, triggering a vicious cycle that will likely keep soccer down—unless an American Pelé or Diego Maradona comes along to bring it to the forefront of the country's consciousness.

In the meantime, sports analysts will continue to puzzle over why Americans don't care about soccer. It's kind of like another vexing sports question: Why do Americans watch NASCAR?

Q Why do golfers wear such silly clothes?

A In most of the major sports, athletes don't have much choice when it comes to what they wear. Basketball, football, baseball, and hockey teams all have uniforms. But other athletes aren't so lucky (and neither are their fans). Golfers, for example, are allowed to choose their own garb, leading to a parade of "uniforms" that look as if they were stitched together by a band of deranged clowns.

Why big-time golfers wear such hideous clothes is a source of bewilderment. Some apologists blame it on the Scots. Golf, after all, was supposedly invented by shepherds in Scotland back in the twelfth century, and it almost goes without saying that a sport born in a country where man-skirts are considered fashionable is doomed from the start. We'd like to point out that we are no longer in twelfth-century Scotland—let's move on, people.

But history may indeed play a role in golf's repeated fashion disasters. Kings and queens were reputed to have hit the links in the sixteenth and seventeenth centuries, and by the late nineteenth century, golf was a popular pastime amongst the nobility of England and Scotland. The nobility, however, wasn't exactly known for its athletic prowess. The other "sports" many of these noblemen participated in were activities like steeplechase (which has its own awful fashion), and so most early golfers had no idea what types of clothes would be appropriate for an athletic endeavor. Early golfers simply took to the links wearing the fashionable attire of the day—attire that, unfortunately, included breeches and ruffled cravats (these were like neckties).

The tradition of wearing stuffy, silly attire continued into the twentieth century (as did the tradition of wealthy, paunchy white guys playing the sport), with awful sweaters and polyester pants replacing the ruffled cravats and knee-length knickers. Yet, remarkably, modern golfers take umbrage at the stereotype that duffers have no sense of fashion. According to one golf wag, the knock on golfers for being the world's worst-dressed athletes is unfair because nowadays almost everybody wears Dockers and polo shirts. (We'll pause while that gem sinks in.)

To be fair, the dreadful golf fashions of the 1970s and 1980s have given way to a more benign blandness that is at least less offensive, if not remotely what anybody would call "stylish." Of course, *all* fashion is less offensive than it was in the 1970s and 1980s, so perhaps golf fashion is proportionally no better.

"Golf," Mark Twain once complained, "is a good walk spoiled." We love Mark Twain, but we have to say that spoiling a good walk is the least of golf's transgressions.

Q Who's the guy on the NBA logo?

A No matter where you are in the world, there is a symbol that almost everyone recognizes. For many people, it represents not just the American sport of basketball, but also all of American sport—and in some ways, perhaps America itself.

No, we're not talking about the Air Jordan logo. We're referring to the NBA logo—you know, the white-silhouetted player who is driving to the hoop over a background of red and blue. But as recognizable as the logo is, you'd be hard-pressed to find many people who can name the guy after which it is modeled.

Well, that guy is Jerry West. Even though most younger fans of the game may think of West as a silver-haired director of basketball operations who represented the Memphis Grizzlies at various draft-lottery drawings, West is one of the greatest guards to ever play the game.

Known as "Mr. Clutch," West averaged twenty-seven points a game during his fourteen-year career with the Los Angeles Lakers. West was an all-star fourteen times, earned several nods to the NBA all-defensive team, and was an All-Star Game and a Finals most valuable player. But more than his statistics or awards, his silky-smooth movements were what prompted NBA logo designer Alan Siegel to model his 1969 design after a photograph of West driving to the hoop.

Despite the iconic nature of the West-inspired logo, there has been a recent movement calling for its redesign. West, these critics say, is too outdated to represent what the NBA is all about right now, and some younger fans don't even know who he is. The most common suggestion is to base the redesign on Michael Jordan. But if you really want to symbolize the NBA as it is perceived now, we'd recommend a silhouette of someone altogether different: a corporate-looking, slightly bored fan sitting in a courtside seat.

Chapter Ten

PEOPLE

Q Are the Hatfields and McCoys still feuding?

A Things just aren't like they used to be. America has gone from a country of hardworking people to a consumer-based society that is driven by greed and empty entertainment. Even our family feuds have lost their integrity. Nowadays, people go on *game shows* to battle it out. Back in the good old days—back when America was *America*—folks just shot each other.

With apologies to Richard Dawson, the former host of the silly game show *Family Feud,* the most famous family feud in American history is that of the Hatfields and the McCoys. In the mid-nineteenth century, these two Appalachian clans settled on opposite sides of the quaintly named Tug Fork, a stream that forms part of the West Virginia–Kentucky border. On the West Virginia side lived the Hatfields, a logging family of fifteen that was headed by "Devil Anse" Hatfield, a former Confederate officer who was none too happy that his state had joined the Union. The McCoys were equally large, with patriarch "Rand'l" McCoy siring thirteen children, although some sources indicate that he fathered sixteen children. For many years, the two families coexisted somewhat peacefully, working together and intermarrying furiously (this was Appalachia, after all).

According to some historians, the trouble began when young Harmon McCoy joined the Union army and fought for the North during the Civil War, an offense for which, upon his return to Tug Fork, he was hunted down and killed by a group of Hatfields. Bad feelings simmered through the 1860s and 1870s. They flared up again when a dispute over ownership of a pig led to another murder, this one committed by the McCoys. But the big trouble didn't really ensue until Roseanna McCoy fell in love with a Hatfield. This backwoods version of *Romeo and Juliet* eventually led to the murders of at least twenty members of the two families.

Though there was a great deal of family feuding in Appalachia during the late nineteenth and early twentieth centuries, no squabble captured America's imagination quite like that of the Hatfields and McCoys. Countless folk songs, books, plays, and movies have been written about the two families, and their depiction as violent, poorly educated, incestuous hillbillies has been instrumental in creating the popular perception of Appalachia. Some might say that the Hatfields and McCoys have done more to destroy Appalachia's image than anybody this side of Ned Beatty's "wooer" in *Deliverance*.

But grudges can only last so long. In 1891, after the fighting got so bad that it was making national headlines, the families finally decided to call a truce. Over the next century, they lived in uneasy harmony. Then in 1979, the Hatfield and McCoy families emerged from their remote Appalachian homes to join the rest of the world—by appearing together on *Family Feud*.

Q Are women smarter than men?

A Not if you consider IQ. According to several studies, men score an average of five points higher than women on intelligence quotient tests. But does this mean that men are smarter than women?

Dr. Paul Irwing and Professor Richard Lynn seem to think so. Based on IQ tests that were administered to some hundred thousand people, the British researchers concluded that there are twice as many men than women with IQ scores of at least 125. (The average human IQ score is one hundred.) Irwing and Lynn also concluded there are five times as many men as women with scores of at least 155, considered "genius" level. The findings were published in the *British Journal of Psychology*, Irwing says that they "may go some way to explaining the greater numbers of men achieving distinctions of various kinds, such as chess grand-masters, Fields medalists for mathematics, Nobel prize-winners and the like."

But how valid is IQ testing in determining whether one sex is smarter than the other?

Even professionally administered IQ tests are primitive measures of intelligence," says Marilyn vos Savant, who has been listed in the *Guinness World Records* under "Highest IQ" for both childhood and adult scores. Vos Savant maintains that intelligence is impossible  to quantify. "So many factors are involved that attempts to measure it are useless," she says. "Not that IQ tests are useless. Far from it. Good tests work: They measure a variety of mental abilities, and the best tests do it well. But they don't measure intelligence itself."

Still, what explains the male-female difference in IQ scores? Irwing and Lynn, along with controversial researchers such as Britain's John Philippe Rushton, claim that it comes down to brain size. "Men have larger brains than women by about 10 percent, and larger brains confer greater brain power, so men must necessarily be on average more intelligent than women," Lynn wrote in a letter to *The Psychologist*. It is important to understand, however, that the same researchers who maintain that men are more intelligent than women also acknowledge that higher IQ scores have few implications in the real world.

Furthermore, although many more men than women score at the very top of the IQ scale, many more men also score at the very bottom. This, observes Savant, "could account for the greater number of men in the sciences and—on the other end—in the prison population."

When former Harvard president Lawrence Summers suggested in 2005 that men outperform women in math and science, partly due to inherent differences in intellectual ability, he sparked an academic uproar. The truth is, women are rapidly overtaking men in both educational and occupational achievement. And brain size aside, even Irwing and Lynn claim that at the same IQ levels, women are able to achieve more than men "possibly because they are more conscientious and better adapted to sustained periods of hard work."

There you have it, guys: Size really doesn't matter.

Q Did the Marlboro man die of lung cancer?

A Yes—twice, in fact. There were, you see, many Marlboro men over the years.

In 1954 Philip Morris hired the famous Leo Burnett advertising agency to revamp the Marlboro filtered cigarette brand, which the company had been marketing to women for thirty years. In light of magazine stories about the hazards of smoking, Philip Morris wanted to offer concerned male smokers the option of a "safe," filtered cigarette.

Leo Burnett launched a campaign featuring cowboys and other masculine figures, and before long Marlboro took off among men. In 1963–64, Philip Morris shifted the campaign exclusively to cowboys, who were usually portrayed by real cowboys. The Marlboro man in Marlboro country became one of the most recognized ad campaigns in history, and Marlboro became the nation's best-selling cigarette brand.

In the spring of 1992, former Marlboro model Wayne McLaren made waves when he announced that he was dying of brain cancer, which had started in his lungs. He told his story at the annual Philip Morris shareholders meeting and to the Massachusetts state legislature, which was considering a bill to increase taxes on cigarettes to fund health education. Soon after, McLaren made an anti-smoking ad, contrasting pictures of his rugged cowboy days with pictures of him near death in the hospital. He died the following June.

McLaren did not appear in many Marlboro ads, and Philip Morris initially claimed it had no knowledge that he had worked for the company. It later recanted, however, and admitted that McLaren had been featured in a series of promotional playing cards. But David McLean, a former Marlboro man who died from lung cancer in 1995, had appeared extensively in Marlboro TV and print ads in the 1960s. In 1996, his widow filed a high-profile lawsuit against Philip Morris and the major tobacco companies, claiming they were responsible for McLean's nicotine addiction that ultimately led to his death. The suit contended that McLean had to smoke up to five packs of cigarettes per take when shooting the Marlboro ads so that the photographers and videographers could get the pictures and footage they needed.

If you were to pick the Marlboro man out of a lineup, it probably would be Darrell Winfield, a former ranch hand who dominated Marlboro billboard and print ads in the 1970s and 1980s. Winfield is reportedly cancer-free, living happily on his ranch in Wyoming. It's not clear whether he still smokes.

Q Was there a real Sherlock Holmes?

A Since bursting onto the scene in 1887, Sherlock Holmes has become quite the celebrity. The members of his fan club, sometimes dubbed the Baker Street Irregulars, number in the hundreds of thousands worldwide. In the twentieth century, many readers were so convinced that Holmes was a real person that they sent mail to his address at 221b Baker Street in London. In the twenty-first century, he has his own page on Facebook.

Holmes is, of course, fictional. But is the detective based on fact? Author Sir Arthur Conan Doyle claimed that he modeled his famous detective on Dr. Joseph Bell (1837–1911) of the University of Edinburgh. Doyle had been Bell's assistant when Doyle was a medical student at the university from 1877 to 1881.

Like everyone else, Doyle was awed by Bell's ability to deduce all kinds of details regarding the geographical origins, life histories, and professions of his patients by his acute powers of observation. The doctor had what his students called "the look of eagles"; little escaped him. Reportedly, he could tell a working man's trade by the pattern of the calluses on his hands and what countries a sailor had visited by his tattoos.

In 1892 Doyle wrote an appreciative letter to his old mentor, saying, "It is most certainly to you that I owe Sherlock Holmes." The resemblance between Bell and Holmes was strong enough to impress Bell's fellow Scotsman Robert Louis Stevenson. After reading several Sherlock Holmes stories in a popular magazine, Stevenson sent a note to Doyle asking, "Can this be my old friend Joe Bell?"

When queried by journalists about the fictitious doppelganger, Bell modestly replied that "Dr. Conan Doyle has, by his imaginative genius, made a great deal out of very little, and his warm remembrance of one of his old teachers has coloured the picture." Nevertheless, Bell was pleased to write an introduction to the 1892 edition of *A Study in Scarlet,* the tale that had launched Holmes's career as a sleuth—and Doyle's as a writer. By the mid-1890s, Doyle had largely abandoned medicine for the life of a full-time writer.

Bell's association with Holmes wasn't his only claim to fame. He was a fellow of the Royal College of Surgeons of Edinburgh, the author of several medical textbooks, and one of the founders of modern forensic pathology. The University of Edinburgh honored his legacy by establishing the Joseph Bell Centre for Forensic Statistics and Legal Reasoning in March 2001.

One of the center's first initiatives was to develop a software program that could aid investigations into suspicious deaths. "It takes an overview of all the available evidence," said Jeroen Keppens, one of the program's developers, "and then speculates on what might have happened." Police detectives have praised the potential of the software, which is called, fittingly, Sherlock Holmes.

Q What's the difference between a nerd and a geek?

A Life was simpler back in the 1950s. If you were a guy named, say, Fonzie—hanging out at the drive-in, donning your leather jacket and slicked-back hair, speaking with a New York accent even though you lived in Milwaukee—you knew you were cool. If you saw some brainiac who went around carrying books and wearing glasses, you could point at him and call him a nerd. And geeks were something else entirely: When you hopped on your motorcycle and went to a carnival to see the tattooed lady and the weirdo biting the head off a live chicken, those wild carnies were true geeks.

People understood their roles and their places in society's pecking order. People understood the labels that had been assigned to them. In short, people knew who was supposed to give the wedgies and who was supposed to receive the wedgies.

Time marched on, and the lines became blurred. In the 1960s, the nerds learned all about computers; in the 1970s and 1980s, they got rich, which meant that they could buy contact lenses and enough black turtlenecks to make themselves look cool. Meanwhile, rock stars started acting like carnival geeks, doing outrageous stuff like biting the heads off of live chickens—yet people considered them cool, too. And those formerly cool guys got old and fat but kept slicking back their hair and going to the drive-in, which wasn't geeky, nerdy, or cool. It was just kind of pathetic— unless they were Elvis impersonators, in which case they teetered on the brink of geekdom.

Then the 1990s arrived, bringing an outburst of irony that lingered into the new century. Computer nerds started referring to themselves as geeks in an effort to seem cool, and people bought it. In order to be really cool, they were almost required to get nerdy glasses and pretend like they didn't care about their hairstyles. And self-mutilation in the form of tattoos and piercings—once the exclusive domain of geeks—became cool

Where have you gone, Arthur Fonzarelli? A nation turns its confused eyes to you.

The fact of the matter is that if there ever was a difference between a nerd and a geek, it has long since been obliterated. "Geek" appears to come from a Germanic word meaning "fool"; it became part of our vocabulary around 1900. "Nerd" entered the lexicon around 1950; it may have been coined by Dr. Seuss in his book of that year, *If I Ran the Zoo.* Grab any dictionary and you'll find that the definitions for both words describe basically the same thing: a person who is unstylish, socially inept, a little too knowledgeable in a particular subject, and generally disliked. The word "computer" shows up a lot in the usage examples.

Merciless ridicule of unfortunate misfits was so much more precise back in the good old days.

Q Who invented the match?

A For thousands of years, "keep the home fires burning" wasn't a cute saying—it was a major undertaking. Once your fire went out, there was no way to start it again except with good old-fashioned friction (i.e., rubbing two sticks together or striking a flint against a rock until you got a light).

Around 1680, Robert Boyle, an chemist from Ireland, discovered that a stick coated with sulfur would ignite instantly when rubbed against a piece of paper coated with phosphorous. But prior to the Industrial Revolution, both sulfur and phosphorous were expensive and hard to produce, so Boyle's discovery had no practical application for nearly one hundred and fifty years.

Real matches appeared on the market in 1827 after John Walker, an English chemist and apothecary, stirred up a mixture of potassium chlorate and antimony sulfide. He coated the end of a stick with this mixture, let it dry, scraped it against sandpaper, and—just like that—fire. Walker named his matchsticks Congreves, after the weaponry rockets that were developed by Sir William Congreve in about 1804. Like rockets, Walker's Congreves often did more harm than good, sending out showers of sparks that lit not just lamps and stoves, but rugs, ladies' dresses, and gentlemen's wigs.

But such calamities didn't deter Samuel Jones, another Englishman. Jones modified Walker's process to make it less explosive, patented the result, and called his product Lucifers, a playful reference to the devilish odor given off by burning sulfide. Despite their nasty stench, Lucifers proved to be a big hit among gentlemen who liked to indulge in the new pastime of smoking cigars.

In an effort to produce an odor-free match, French chemist Charles Sauria added white phosphorous to the sulfur mixture in 1830. Unfortunately, white phosphorous not only killed the smell, but it also killed those who made the matches. Thousands of the young women and children who worked in match factories began to suffer from phossy jaw, a painful and fatal bone disease caused by chronic exposure to the fumes of white phosphorous. (Once white phosphorous was understood to be poisonous, reformers worked to ban it from matches, finally succeeding with the Berne Convention of 1906, an international treaty that prohibited its use in manufacture and trade.)

In the 1850s, Swedish brothers John "Johan" and Carl Lundstrom created a match that was coated with red instead of white phosphorous on the striking surface. Red phosphorous was more expensive, but unlike its pale cousin, it was nontoxic when inhaled.

Over the next sixty years, inventors experimented with many types of red phosphorous matches, the best being the "safety" matches that were patented by the Diamond Match Company of the United States in 1910. President William Howard Taft was so impressed by the company's new matches that he asked Diamond to make its patent available to everyone "for the good of all mankind." On January 28, 1911, Diamond complied, and ever since, the match business has been booming. You might say it's spread like wildfire.

Q Why do the Amish keep telephones outside their homes?

A The Amish are an integral part of highway billboard culture and handcrafted furniture lore throughout Pennsylvania and parts of the Midwest. Some people know them from the 1985 Harrison Ford movie *Witness*. You remember that one, right? Ford works undercover in an Amish community to crack a murder case. Still blanking? Kelly McGillis gives herself a sponge bath. Ah, *now* it's coming back to you.

Anyway, as the movie also depicts, the Amish are a community of veritable Luddites, eschewing modern technology for the simpler pleasures of horses, buggies, and sweet, sweet beards. So the question isn't so much, "Why do Amish keep telephones outside their homes?" It's, "Why do the Amish keep telephones anywhere?"

To answer this, we'll need to understand a little bit more about the Amish than Harrison Ford films or country cookin' ads can offer. The Amish are part of a larger religious group known as the Anabaptists, which also include Mennonites and Brethren sects. In the late seventeenth century, Jakob Ammann, a Mennonite from Switzerland, led a split from the larger Mennonite church. (He felt it was getting too undisciplined.) By the early eighteenth century, members of his sect—known as the Amish—were coming to America to escape religious persecution, eventually settling in southeastern Pennsylvania.

Though the religious differences between Amish and other Christians are somewhat arcane, the Amish's views on culture and technology are what capture the public imagination. These beliefs stem from a central guiding principle known as *Gelassenheit*—no, it's not what the Amish say when someone sneezes—that roughly means "yielding completely to God's will." Because the Amish see family structure, prayer, humility, and pacifism as the means to *Gelassenheit,* possessing most types of technology is banned. The belief is that modern-day gadgets distract people from their families and God.

Many Amish orders, how-ever, do allow the limited

use of technology (which is why you may see Amish flying on planes or taking trains). This is where telephones come in. When telephones were introduced to the Amish in the late nineteenth century, they were looked at with severe disapproval. Elders were concerned with the lascivious messages younger Amish might pass along to each other over the privacy of the phone lines, and they also worried about the spiritual implications of this "magic" form of communication.

Around 1910, the Amish community officially banned the ownership of telephones. But though the Amish may be stuck in the old ways, they aren't stupid Telephones are incredibly practical devices, especially in the rural areas where the Amish usually live. That's why Amish leaders didn't ban the *use* of telephones. They allow community phones: single telephones kept in wooden shacks and shared by a number of families. These phones usually have unlisted numbers and are used for emergencies, not chit-chatting with the neighbors.

But perhaps the most important reason the Amish allow telephones in the community is also the most obvious: How else are they going to call their friends when Harrison Ford shows up to help them raise a barn?

Q What's the difference between a mass murderer and serial killer?

A Serial killers are made of sugar and spice and everything nice, and mass murderers are...wait, that's not right. The distinction is actually very simple.

A mass murderer kills four or more people during a short period of time, usually in one location. In most cases, the murderer has a sudden mental collapse and goes on a rampage, progressing from murder to murder without a break. About half the time, these outbreaks end in suicides or fatal standoffs with the police. Various school shootings over the years have been instances of mass murder, as have been famous cases of postal workers, well, "going postal." A case in which someone murders his or her entire family is a mass murder. Terrorists are lumped into this category as well, but they also make up a group of their own.

A serial killer usually murders one person at a time (typically a stranger), with a "cooling off" period between each transgression. Unlike mass murderers, serial killers don't suddenly snap one day—they have an ongoing compulsion (usually with a sexual component) that drives them to kill, often in very specific ways. They may even maintain jobs and normal relationships while going to great lengths to conceal their killings. They may resist the urge to kill for long periods, but the compulsion ultimately grows too strong to subjugate. After the third victim, an aspiring killer graduates from plain ol' murderer to bona fide serial killer.

In between these two groups, we have the spree killer and the serial spree killer. A spree killer commits murder in multiple locations over the course of a few days. This is often part of a general crime wave. For example, an escaped convict may kill multiple people, steal cars, jaywalk, and litter as he tries to escape the police. As with a mass murderer, a spree killer doesn't plan each murder individually.

The serial spree killer, on the other hand, plans and commits each murder separately, serial-killer style. But he or she doesn't take time off between murders or maintain a double life. It's all killing, all the time. One of the best-known examples is the Washington, D.C.-area beltway snipers who killed ten people within three weeks in October 2002.

Of course, if you see any of these types of killer in action, don't worry about remembering the right term when you call the police. They're all equally bad.

Q Who started the best-seller list for books?

A Ever read *Beside the Bonnie Brier Bush*? Never even heard of it? Chances are that you're not alone. But in 1895, this forgotten novel by Scotsman Ian Maclaren topped the first list of best-selling books in the United States.

Compiled by editor Harry Thurston Peck for *The Bookman* magazine's February issue, the list reflected sales from a number of major bookstores throughout the country. He presented his list as books sold "in order of demand." The phrase "best-selling" was not used until 1897. Thurston probably got his idea from *The Bookman*'s sister publication in Britain, which had started querying bookstores about their sales in 1891. The British *The Bookman,* however, only listed the most popular books cited by booksellers in different regions of the country. The editors did not combine the statistics to come up with the top book in the nation.

Whether you're talking infielders or authors, there's something uniquely American about the desire to know who's *numero uno.*

Publishers Weekly, the book trade's bible, started its best-seller list in 1912. The editors went *The Bookman* one better by adding a second list for nonfiction. What topped *PW's* first lists? Gene Stratton Porter's novel about the Midwest, *The Harvester,* and Bostonian Mary Antin's memoir of her immigrant youth, *The Promised Land,* headed the fiction and nonfiction lists, respectively.

Today, the *New York Times'* best-seller list is considered to be the gold standard. But the newspaper didn't get into the best-seller game until 1942. Not surprisingly, nonfiction readers were scooping up books with wartime themes that year: Elliot Paul's paean to the city of lights, *The Last Time I Saw Paris,* headed the list—it was followed by *They Were Expendable,* the story of a real-life torpedo boat squadron in the Pacific, by W. L. White; and *Victory Through Air Power,* by Russian-American aviation pioneer Alexander de Seversky.

It's easy to see from the titles we've mentioned that topping the best-seller list is no guarantee of immortality. For every *Gone with the Wind* (best-seller, 1936–37) and *Bonfire of the Vanities* (1988), there are dozens of former hits that are gathering dust on library shelves. Still, the lists provide snapshots of popular culture in given years. For instance, Jacqueline Susann's *Valley of the Dolls* says a lot about what was on America's mind in 1966 (sex, drugs, and more sex and drugs); Stephen King's *It* speaks to 1986 (sex and the supernatural); and John Grisham's *The Broker* is an ode to 2005 (sex, money, and more sex and money).

See some winning themes? Sex, sprinkled with drugs, money, and the supernatural. Run with any or all of these topics, and perhaps tomorrow's top spot on the best-seller list will be yours.

Q Whatever happened to D. B. Cooper?

A On the day before Thanksgiving, 1971, in Portland, Oregon, a man in his mid-forties who called himself Dan Cooper (news reports would later misidentify him as "D. B.") boarded a Northwest Orient Airlines 727 that was bound for Seattle. Dressed in a suit and tie and carrying a briefcase, Cooper was calm and polite when he handed a note to a flight attendant. The note said that his briefcase contained a bomb; he was hijacking the plane. Cooper told the crew that upon landing in Seattle, he wanted four parachutes and two hundred thousand dollars in twenty-dollar bills.

His demands were met, and Cooper released the other passengers. He ordered the pilots to fly to Mexico, but he gave specific instructions to keep the plane under ten thousand feet with the wing flaps at fifteen degrees, restricting the aircraft's speed. That night, in a cold rainstorm somewhere over southwest Washington, Cooper donned the parachutes, and with the money packed in knapsacks that were tied to his body, he jumped from the 727's rear stairs.

For several months afterward, the FBI conducted an extensive manhunt of the rugged forest terrain, but the agents were unable to find even a shred of evidence. In 1972, a copycat hijacker named Richard McCoy successfully jumped from a flight over Utah with five hundred thousand dollars and was arrested days later. At first the FBI thought McCoy was Cooper, but he didn't match the description provided by the crew of Cooper's flight. Other suspects surfaced over the years, including a Florida antiques dealer with a shady past who confessed to his wife on his deathbed that he was Cooper—though he was later discredited by DNA testing.

Cooper hadn't hurt anybody, and he had no apparent political agenda. He became a folk hero of sorts—he was immortalized in books, in song, in television documentaries, and in a movie, *The Pursuit of D.B. Cooper*. In 1980, solid evidence surfaced: An eight-year-old boy found $5,800 in rotting twenty-dollar bills along the Columbia River, and the serial numbers matched those on the cash that was given to Cooper. But while thousands of leads have been investigated over the years, the case remains the only unsolved hijacking in U.S. history. Late in 2007, the FBI's Seattle field office kick-started the investigation, providing pictures on its Web site of some key evidence, including the money and Cooper's black clip-on tie.

Agent Larry Carr continues to work the case. He, like agents who came before him, believes he knows what happened to Cooper, who jumped into a wind of two hundred miles per hour in total darkness on a cold and rainy night. "Diving into the wilderness without a plan, without the right equipment, in such terrible conditions," Carr says, "he probably never even got his chute open."

Q Who told the first knock-knock joke?

A No one really knows for sure, but it couldn't have happened before the wooden door was invented, right? Could the "Knock, knock! Who's there?" phenomenon have started with the ancient Egyptians? According to historians, Egyptian genius was concentrated in the fields of mathematics, medicine, and architecture—not corny comedy.

As old and tired as knock-knock jokes may seem, they appear to be a fairly recent development. In August 1936, *Variety,* a trade magazine covering the entertainment industry, reported that a "knock knock craze" was sweeping America. Around the same time, British comedian Wee Georgie Wood debuted the catchphrase "knock, knock!" on his radio show. (It wasn't the setup to a joke, but a warning that a zinger was about to come.)

The knock-knock joke may have evolved from a Victorian party game called "knock, knock." According to language historian Joseph Twadell Shipley, the game started when a partygoer knocked on the door: "Who's there?" "Buff." "Buff who?" "Buff you!" The "buff" then tried to make the other guests laugh with wordplay or slapstick humor. ("Buff" in this sense is connected with "buffoon.") Whoever laughs first became the next buff, and the game began anew.

But the roots of the knock-knock joke may go deeper than this dreadful-sounding party game. In fact, some people credit William Shakespeare for inspiring the pun's classic pattern. How so? Dust off your old copy of *Macbeth* and turn to Act II, Scene 3. That's where you'll find Shakespeare's famous "porter scene," a satiric monologue delivered by a drunken porter who is pretending to be a doorman at the gates of hell:

> Knock, knock, knock. Who's there, i'th' name of Belzebub?—
> Here's a farmer, that hang'd himself on th' expectation of
> plenty: come in, time-pleaser...[*knocking*] Knock, knock.
> Who's there, i'th' other devil's name?—Faith, here's an equivo-

cator, that could swear in both the scales against either scale; who committed treason enough for God's sake, yet could not equivocate to heaven: O! come in, equivocator. [*knocking*] Knock, knock, knock. Who's there?—Faith, here's an English tailor come hither for stealing out of a French hose: come in, tailor; here you may roast your goose.

Of course, today's knock-knock jokes aren't quite as clever or dramatic as Shakespeare's prose, but that may be their draw. Knock-knock jokes are simple wordplays that don't require a whole lot of thinking. And no matter how bad they might be—and they're usually really, really, really bad—they always get a reaction.

Orange you glad we didn't say banana? Sorry—we just couldn't resist that one.

Q Why do grown men still need toys?

A Every Christmas, a scene like this one unfolds in households across America: The kids wake up at the crack of dawn. Silently, with anticipation and bated breath, they creep downstairs to see what Santa has left them. They hear noises in the living room—clicks and rasps, a murmur. Is it possible that Santa is still there? They reach the doorway, peek in, to find...Dad, playing with the video game system that was supposed to be for the kids. Come on, Dad!

Of course, it's commonly held wisdom that most men are just big kids at heart. And like kids, they need their toys, whether their playthings are video games, smart-phones, or sports cars. But why is this? After all, everybody knows that the adult world is a sober, stressful place with no room for childish games.

Maybe not. Play theorists (yes, they really exist) suggest that toys and games aid mental development in children and adults alike. For children, games act as staging grounds for the adult world. (They require cognitive skills like understanding rules or strategy, and social skills like cooperation and communication.) But this development doesn't stop at adulthood. According to scientists, playing with toys can help "potentiate novelty" (This is a fancy way of saying that it can inspire creativity, generate new ideas, and help adults approach problems in new ways.) In fact, Albert Einstein himself stated that play is essential to any productive thought. And who's going to argue with him?

But why do men seem more apt to play with toys than women? While the reasons haven't been extensively studied, one explanation may lie in the respective roles that men and women have traditionally played in society. For most of modern history, men have been the wage-earners, the handlers of weighty responsibilities—the very ones for whom "potentiating novelty" is the most important. And as bacon-bringers and novelty-potentiators, they deserve nothing less than a hot meal when they get home from the office, a nice martini, and, obviously, a sixteen-thousand-dollar stereo system. A woman, on the other hand, is trained by society to play the role of caregiver, of homemaker, of nurturer. There is no time—or excuse—for frivolity when the laundry needs washing, the kids need bathing, and the husband's martini needs mixing.

Of course, some people—husbands, mainly—might call this assumption a load of B.S. After all, isn't an eight-hundred-dollar

Prada handbag a type of toy? Regardless, as gender roles continue to evolve, there may be a correlating shift in how men and women approach leisure. And this may be a good thing for everybody because—in addition to their sociological importance—toys may also have health benefits.

Being an adult can be stressful—and stress, doctors tell us, is one of the worst things for our bodies. Enter toys. Play therapists suggest that one of the best ways for reducing stress is to hit the arcade or pick up a hobby. In fact, an intense game of air-hockey at that arcade may have health benefits beyond mere stress reduction. Indeed, mounting evidence suggests that active use of the brain—through the creative thinking or puzzle-solving involved with many computer games, for example—may help stave off degenerative brain diseases like Alzheimer's. This is good news for the 53 percent of adults who reported to the Pew Center in 2008 that they routinely play video games.

So go ahead, Dad—it's okay to play a little Xbox on Christmas morning. Just give the kids a turn once in a while.

Q How many Ronald McDonalds have there been?

A McDonald's guards this bit of information even more closely than its secret sauce recipe. The company won't even acknowledge the existence of multiple Ronalds, though McDonald's obviously would need many actors to keep up with store openings, hospital visits, and other events around the world. The company forbids Ronald actors from revealing what they do.

The only specific Ronald actor that McDonald's happily acknowledges is the original one, Willard Scott, who went on to become the world's most famous weatherman. The story began in 1960, when Scott played Bozo the Clown in the Washington, D.C., version of *Bozo's Circus*. A local McDonald's franchisee sponsored the show, and Scott also appeared as Bozo at McDonald's restaurants as part of the promotion. He was a big hit, so when the station dropped *Bozo's Circus* in 1963, a franchisee hired Scott to play a new McDonald's clown character in local ads.

The ads were a success, and McDonald's decided in 1965 to feature the character in nationwide TV spots as part of its sponsorship of the Macy's Thanksgiving Day parade. Instead of using Scott, McDonald's hired a thinner actor, reasoning that it would be easier to find lean actors rather than heavy actors to play Ronald around the nation. (Guess the obesity epidemic hadn't yet gripped America.)

The history gets fuzzy there, but we know that McDonald's was working through the 1970s on building its clown army. In 1972 the company published *Ronald and How,* a training manual for new Ronalds. In a 2003 *Wall Street Journal* article, marketing experts who were familiar with McDonald's said that there were about two hundred and fifty active Ronalds around the world, which could mean that there have been several thousand over the years. Every two years, current Ronalds and prospective Ronalds attend a secret Ronald McDonald convention, where they have to pass inspection. It's heady stuff, to be sure.

Scott is the only person confirmed by McDonald's to have appeared as Ronald in television ads. There are Internet rumors about other TV Ronalds, but these actors are unconfirmed. Mayor McCheese could not be reached for comment.

Q Are there really only "six degrees" separating you from any other person?

A The idea isn't as far-fetched as you might think. The "six degrees" theory holds that through no more than five mutual acquaintances, you can reach anybody on the planet. For example, you might get to the Queen of England because your cousin did time with a roadie who toured with Paul McCartney, who's tight with the Queen because she knighted him.

The notion first popped up in a 1929 book of short stories by Hungarian writer Frigyes Karinthy. In one story, a character suggests that he could connect to anybody with no more than five people between them. In 1967, a Harvard professor named Stanley Milgram put this notion to the test. He sent letters to several hundred randomly selected people in Kansas and Nebraska, giving each person the name and basic description of someone in Massachusetts. Each participant was supposed to send the letter to an acquaintance who might be closer to the final target; all of the participants along the chain mailed postcards back to Harvard to signal that they had passed on the letter. One letter got to the target in only two steps, though others took almost a dozen steps; Milgram claimed that the median was 5.5 steps. John Guare referenced the idea in his 1990 play *Six Degrees of Separation* (which was made into a movie in 1993), and the term became famous.

Two Cornell researchers were inspired to attack the question mathematically. In a study published in 1998, they explained the fundamental qualities of a "small-world" network. If you picture the human social network graphically, with people as points and relationships as lines between the points, you naturally get ordered clusters of interconnected dots—a lot of the people in your social circle and residential area know each other or are only one mutual acquaintance away from each other. This is an *ordered* network. But there is an element of randomness—the odd connection to someone who's well outside the cluster. This is a *disordered* network. The researchers found that if a small percentage of connections in a mostly ordered network are random—that is, connections between points that go outside ordered clusters—you create shortcuts all over the network. This can make any individual point only a small number of connections away from any other.

For example, if you've always lived in Detroit, most of your friends probably live in Motown, too. Collectively, you form a cluster of many interconnected people. But let's say that your cousin's college roommate lives in Mumbai, India. Through that link, you're connected to a cluster of people in India, and—through you—so is everyone you know in Detroit. And since all of these people have their own random connections, you end up being linked to clusters all over the world. According to the researcher's model, if only 1 percent of all connections in a network are this sort of random leap between clusters, any two points (e.g., people) end up being closely connected. This is the same basic phenomenon that connects the hundred billion neurons in your brain.

This study, and others like it, shows that there might indeed be only six degrees separating you from any other person. Find the right connections, and you'll be enjoying high tea with the Queen.

Chapter Eleven

ORIGINS

Q **How long is a New York minute?**

A New Yorkers have a reputation for being rude, provincial, haughty, and hurried—and for good reason. They won't hesitate to tell you that there are no bagels like New York bagels, no delis like New York like delis, no theaters like Broadway theaters, no avenues like Fifth Avenue, and no teams like the Yankees. New Yorkers even seem to believe that their units of time are superior to the pedestrian measurements the rest of us use. Think a minute lasts sixty seconds? Not in New York.

Sometimes a minute can seem like a pretty long time. Try holding your breath for a minute. Or holding a sack of cement. Or watching an episode of *Grey's Anatomy.* Or speaking with a New Yorker. And sometimes the word "minute" merely signifies a short, indefinite period of time—consider how we use the word colloquially, as in, "I'll be back in a minute" or "I was into that band for, like, a minute." The phrase "New York minute" carries a similar meaning.

Ironically, it doesn't appear as if New Yorkers coined the phrase. According to most etymologists, it probably originated in Texas. The disdain of Texans for New Yorkers (or just about any city slickers) might be thinly masked, but "New York minute" isn't really that much of an insult.

In popular usage, it merely means a short unit of time, possibly playing on the idea that life in New York City is hectic and a minute in the hurried atmosphere of the Big Apple passes more quickly than in the rest of the world. How fast? Well, according to the *Galveston News,* where the phrase first appeared in print in 1954, a New York minute lasts about thirty seconds.

But a New York minute might be even shorter than that. As Johnny Carson once put it, a New York minute is the amount of time that lapses between the light changing to green and the jerk behind you starting to honk.

Q Why is blue for boys and pink for girls?

A There are two views on the subject, and as you might expect, they're as different as the two colors.

Some experts believe that it comes down to innate preferences. In a study published in 2007, two researchers at Newcastle University in England suggested that women are biologically predisposed to like shades of red. They recruited 208 people who were in their early twenties and had each pick a favorite color from a series of choices. Overall, both men and women liked shades of blue the best, though women also gravitated to shades of red.

The participants were mostly British Caucasians, but researchers also included thirty-seven Chinese men and women in the study in order to gauge the influence of cultural norms. Red was the most popular with both Chinese women and men (it's considered a lucky color in China), but Chinese women did show a special preference for pink.

The researchers suggested that a fondness for shades of red would have benefited our primitive female ancestors, who spent their days gathering reddish fruits and berries while the males hunted. Additionally, they theorized, females may have developed a greater sensitivity to shades of red in order to gauge the degrees of a fever in a baby. The researchers posited that both genders naturally like blue because of the blue sky we associate with good weather.

This is a neat story, but it's only conjecture. The limited scope of the study leaves a lot of room for the alternate view: that color preference is purely cultural. History is in agreement here. The notion of separate colors for male and female babies didn't emerge at all until the latter part of the nineteenth century. Before then, boys and girls both usually wore white (and both wore frilly dresses, incidentally).

It's not clear who first thought of color-coding babies, but it may have been the French. The 1868 novel *Little Women* refers to the use of a blue ribbon for a boy twin and a pink ribbon for a girl twin, in "French fashion." The idea slowly spread in Britain and in the United States, but for many years, nobody could agree on which color went with which gender. In fact, many people may have done the opposite of today's standard.

For example, a 1918 edition of *Ladies' Home Journal* article said: "There has been a great diversity of opinion on the subject, but the generally accepted rule is pink for the boy and blue for the girl. The reason is that pink being a more decided and stronger color is more suitable for the boy, while blue, which is more delicate and dainty, is prettier for the girl."

But things changed in the 1950s—Americans universally adopted pink as a feminine color. Some researchers attribute this to a college fad: In 1948, young ladies began wearing pink men's shirts from Brooks Brothers, which apparently sparked a wider love of pink among women.

And, of course, once all of the women started donning the color, the guys moved their pink clothes to the dark recesses of their closets.

Q Do you need a brush to paint the town red?

A You can bring a brush if you want to, but a wad of cash and a few friends will probably serve you better, because painting the town red means going out and having a wild time. The phrase is often used by people who have cause to celebrate: "Let's go out and paint the town red!"

How did painting become associated with raucous partying, and why red? One explanation dates back to England in 1837, when the Marquis of Waterford and some of his friends are said to have wreaked a little havoc in a town called Melton Mowbray; apparently, as part of their revelry, they painted some public buildings a crimson hue. Those wacky Brits! As fun as that sounds, it's unlikely that it accounts for the true origin of the phrase. The earliest published references are from the 1880s, and they all occurred in the United States.

One explanation posits that the saying may have come out of the nineteenth-century Wild West, where the unseemly parts of a town (i.e., the places where people had the most fun) were referred to as red-light districts. Lusty revelers who were ready for a night of no-holds-barred action may have vowed to carry their craziness anywhere they pleased, thereby making the entire town a red-light district. This explanation seems to involve more fun than the story of our friend the Marquis, but it calls for less actual paint.

The problem with identifying the origin of a phrase that is used to describe a night of drunken debauchery is that your average drunken debaucher tends to forget a lot of what happened during said debauchery. For this reason, we'll probably never know precisely how the term was coined.

So, no, you don't need a brush to paint the town red, but it's definitely a good idea to use a toothbrush the next morning.

Q Was eating cold turkey ever a treatment for addiction?

A Americans eat a lot of turkey at Thanksgiving—almost seven hundred million pounds, in fact. Of course, only a fraction of that is eaten on the holiday itself. The rest is parceled out in various leftover forms over the following weeks: turkey sandwiches, turkey chili, turkey smoothies. In the midst of this onslaught, it might be natural to wonder just how the meat is connected to the idiom "going cold turkey." We can imagine cold turkey being a cure for a number of things—such as, by week three of leftovers, an excessive appetite—but drug addiction has never been one of them.

The phrase "cold turkey," which refers to an addiction treatment that involves simply quitting the vice altogether, has been around in print since at least the 1920s, but it may actually be older. The debate over its origin is as hotly contested as the battle over the Thanksgiving wishbone. A favorite colloquial explanation suggests that "cold turkey" evolved from the slang of drug addicts to refer to the symptoms of withdrawal. Because a classic symptom of drug withdrawal is goose bumps, caused by massive chills, it is said that the flesh of a recovering addict resembles that of a plucked turkey. It's an interesting explanation, but it probably isn't rooted in fact.

Most etymologists suggest that "cold turkey" evolved from an older phrase: "talk turkey." Though this term isn't used much anymore, your great-grandparents may remember people saying it when they wanted to get to the point. A variation of the phrase "talk turkey" was "talk cold turkey," which was, apparently, an even simpler and more direct way to broach a subject. It doesn't take a huge leap in logic to see how this could be applied to the realm of addiction.

Going cold turkey after Thanksgiving means something entirely different. And things don't get much better after Christmas, when we're forced to go cold ham.

Q Did Indians really take back gifts?

A History, it is said, is told by the conqueror. The same goes for figures of speech. English is rife with phrases that put down other cultures—as one would expect, considering that England and the United States have, by and large, played the role of conqueror over the past two hundred years.

So it is perhaps no surprise that Dutch couples don't really split the bill; French people don't run around sticking their tongues in each other's mouths; and Indians, despite what you learned on the grade-school playground, never participated in the practice of giving gifts and then demanding them back.

The term "Indian giver" has a long history—almost as long as white people have been in contact with Native Americans. But the phrase wasn't always used as it is now. It first appeared in print in Thomas Hutchinson's 1765 tome *The History of the Province of Massachusetts Bay.* Hutchinson called an "Indian gift" a "proverbial expression, signifying a present for which an equivalent return is expected." This definition is rooted in a fundamental misunderstanding of certain Native American economies, which were based on trade and barter, as well as gift-giving practices (such as exchanges of gifts of equal or greater values). But to the Europeans, expecting something in return for a gift was uncivilized.

The term "Indian giver" took on the connotation of somebody who gave a gift and expected something of equal value in return; if this expectation wasn't met, the gift was taken back. Eventually, the part about expecting something in return was dropped, and an Indian giver became somebody who giveth and then taketh away.

When considering the history of interactions between whites and natives in North America, it's perhaps not surprising that—according to some etymologists—there are many idioms that denigrate Native Americans by using the term "Indian" as a signifier for something fraudulent or of lesser quality. This explains our idioms "Indian summer" and "Indian corn" (but not, as far as we know, the mascot for the Cleveland baseball team, though long-suffering Indians fans may disagree).

Of course, if our idioms were based on historical accuracy, we'd probably have a term for somebody who provides the gift of indiscriminate slaughter, dislocation, promise-breaking, and massive smallpox epidemics: "white-man giver."

Q Why are women called "broads"?

A There's no shortage of nicknames for the fairer sex. They can run from vaguely objectifying to outright vulgar. It's not too difficult to think of several current slang terms that are more offensive than "broad," but in its heyday, it probably packed about as much punch as the more pungent words that are bandied about today.

The earliest documented reference to women as broads appears in a 1914 book of criminal slang. We're guessing that the criminals of 1914 weren't any fonder of delicate poetic nuance than the criminals of today, so it's pretty safe to assume that "broad" had derogatory connotations at that time.

But the origin of the term is not entirely clear. Some people believe that it comes from the phrase "broad in the beam," which originally referred to the width of a ship but was later used to describe a person whose hips and posterior were wider than usual. Or it could have come from the archaic term "abroadwife," which referred to a woman who was away from her husband, typically a slave.

From there, the possibilities slip further toward the pejorative, with prostitution playing a predictably prominent role. One theory holds that "broad" is a variant of "bawd," an Elizabethan-era word for a woman who ran a brothel. Yet another holds that it evolved from an eighteenth-century usage of "broad" that meant "ticket," like a ticket for admission. Pimps allegedly began referring to their prostitutes as "broads," meaning that these women were their meal tickets.

Wherever it came from and however disrespectful it may once have been, "broad" now seems almost quaint, straight out of the vernacular of a fading generation of old, cigar-chomping men who wore fedoras.

Q Did accountants ever actually count beans?

A "The bean counters are coming." It's a sentence that sparks antipathy and fear, evoking an image of a grim-faced, briefcase-toting army of accountants ready to pillage your office with an arsenal of calculators and balance sheets. But just how did accountants come to be known as "bean counters," anyway?

Beans have long had negative connotations—and not just because they're the fruit that makes you toot. Think about it: The phrase "He doesn't know beans" suggests that someone is clueless, and "It doesn't amount to a hill of beans" means that something is meaningless or worthless. You would be hard-pressed, then, to find anything more boring or joyless than counting beans, which is partially why accountants are associated with this label.

One anecdotal explanation posits that the unflattering nickname originated in the 1920s, when the marketing and sales analysis firm the Nielsen Company (now better known for its television ratings system) was just a fledgling operation. The story goes that founder A. C. Nielsen was so diligent in his analysis that his employees counted the beans one by one at grocery stores they were auditing.

This would have been an unimaginably excruciating exercise. And while this explanation certainly seems apt, it's probably not true, especially because the preferred unit of a crop economy is the bushel, not individual grains, seeds, ears, or legumes.

The term "bean counter" first surfaced in a 1975 *Forbes* article, in reference to a particularly careful accountant. It expanded to mean any accountant and then took on a negative implication, suggesting that accountants overlook value for numbers.

Today the term is used to describe any soulless individual who cares more about the bottom line than quality. In other words: "The bean counters in the corner offices have decided that you're expendable." It's little wonder that no one likes the bean counters.

Q What does the "H" stand for in Jesus H. Christ?

A No religion is filled with more arguments, defenses, explanations, proofs, axioms, theorems, and treatises than Christianity. For hundreds of years, the Western world's greatest philosophical and theological minds have wrestled with such soul-saving questions as the nature of the Trinity and the fate of a stillborn's soul. Untold numbers of scholars, millions of pages, and billions of words have been devoted to the explication and illumination of the spiritual fate of humanity.

Yet there is one question that remains unanswered. It is so weighty and so monumental that none of the greatest theological minds in history—not Saint Augustine, not Thomas Aquinas, not Martin Luther—have had the skill or courage to even broach it. This question, of course, is: What does the "H" stand for in Jesus H. Christ?

Fortunately, we're here to answer the truly important questions in life. "Jesus H. Christ," as most of us know firsthand, is a mild expletive. The phrase is rather versatile—it's handy in moments of frustration, anger, astonishment, and bemusement—and the "H" adds a whimsical touch.

Where this oath comes from, though, is a matter of debate. Although the phrase seems somewhat modern in sensibility (and, in fact, didn't first appear in print until the late nineteenth century), no less an authority on language than Mark Twain said that Jesus H. Christ was already well established by 1850. Various explanations for the origin of the "H" have been proffered. Logic dictates that the "H" would stand for "holy" or "hallowed" (as in, "Our Father, who art in heaven, hallowed be thy name...."), but logic and Christianity don't always go hand in hand.

Most language scholars believe the "H" is the result of a misunderstanding of the Greek abbreviation for Jesus's name. The word for Jesus in Greek is *Iesous,* and in many Greek artifacts, this name was shortened to the abbreviation *iota, eta, sigma, IES.* The capital letter form of the Greek letter *eta* resembles the Roman capital letter *H,* and so the average person who was used to the Roman alphabet would have been forgiven if he or she mistakenly believed that the middle letter was indeed *H.*

Of course, we here at F.Y.I. headquarters are about as morally pure a group as you'll ever find, which is why we never take the good Lord's name in vain. This is another, rarely discussed benefit of the middle initial: Since Jesus Christ doesn't really have a middle name, saying "Jesus H. Christ" doesn't *technically* count as taking the Lord's name in vain. And we're working on a six-thousand-page apologia to prove it.

Q Does the squeaky wheel always get the grease?

A Of course. When you arrive at the grocery store on Saturday afternoon to do some shopping in the company of several hundred of your closest friends, you grab the last cart available and immediately understand why nobody else took it: Three of the wheels work, but the fourth emits a deafening shriek with even the slightest movement. "The squeaky wheel *doesn't* always get the grease," you mutter to yourself as you try to wrestle the cart down the aisle. "Who thought of that stupid saying?"

Meanwhile, the little old lady who walked in after you tracks down the nearest stock boy and demands to have a cart retrieved for her. The sulking teen complies and brings her a quiet, perfectly operational cart—the Cadillac of shopping carts. Your problem is that you're too literal. If you had left that cart where it was and done some squeaking like that little old lady did, you would have gotten some grease, too.

It's difficult to pin down the origin of the phrase. Variations—like "the brokenest wheele of the chariot maketh alwaies the greatest noise" (just kidding)—have been in use in English for more than six hundred years. Credit for our version of the saying goes to the aptly named Henry Wheeler Shaw. Writing under the pseudonym Josh Billings, he penned this poem, called "The Kicker" (which was a nineteenth-century term for someone who complains):

> *I hate to be a kicker,*
> *I always long for peace,*
> *But the wheel that does the squeaking,*
> *Is the one that gets the grease.*

Q How does the cat get out of the bag?

A If you've let the cat out of the bag, you've divulged a secret—you've probably ruined what was supposed to be Aunt Miriam's surprise sixtieth birthday party. But just what do cats and bags have to do with spilling the beans?

The origin of this feline-related phrase likely dates to medieval England in the fifteen hundreds. Back then, it was common for merchants to sell goods such as produce and livestock at markets or fairs. When someone bought a live piglet at a market, the merchant would place the animal in a sack so that the purchaser could get the goods home.

Problem was, sometimes those market merchants were less than upstanding. Instead of filling the sack with a valuable piglet, a merchant might try to pass off a useless cat. If (and really, when) that cat was let out of the bag, the merchant's secret was exposed. Of course, anyone who has tried to put a live cat in bag knows that it's only a matter of seconds before that confined kitty will make a rather explosive exit. And doesn't that make sense? Secrets can be really hard to keep!

Sure, we can play dumb, lie, or politely refuse to tell. But in the end, we're all human, and we all seem to share this universal need to share our knowledge, experiences, and feelings with other people. (And sometimes isn't it worth it just to see those stunned looks of shock and utter stupefaction?)

Daniel Wegner, a Harvard psychology professor who has studied the science behind secrets, says, "We don't realize that in keeping a secret, we've created an obsession in a jar." So try as you might to keep that cat in the bag, it's probably going to find its way out. Sorry, Aunt Miriam.

Q Were grapevines ever used to transmit gossip?

A We love our gossip. Tabloids devote entire columns to society rumors, while the water cooler acts as gossip-central in office buildings around the globe. Countless Web sites track celebrity gossip, ESPN has turned into a sports-gossip network, and we even have *Gossip Girl,* a wildly popular television show that celebrates rumor, innuendo, misinformation, and backbiting. But perhaps the most effective way of getting one's gossip is also the oldest: through the grapevine.

Indeed, word-of-mouth gossip has been a part of life since time immemorial. The Greeks even had a goddess of gossip—it had to be a goddess, didn't it?—known as Pheme. (To the Romans she was Fama, from the same root as our "fame.") Sometime around the eighth century BC, the poet Hesiod said, "Do as I tell you— keep away from the gossip of people. For Pheme is an evil thing by nature.... Pheme never disappears entirely once many people have talked her big."

It's tempting, considering the fondness the Greeks had for the fermented nectar of the vine, to believe that the phrase "through the grapevine" was coined because gossip-mongering was connected to their predilection for loosing tongues with the aid of wine. But in fact, the origin is much more recent and the inspiration is entirely different. In 1844 Samuel F. B. Morse invented his telegraph, revolutionizing human communication by allowing messages to travel between far-flung places almost instantly. Of course, we already had a less precise but equally powerful form of long-distance communication: gossip.

In 1852 a book on American politics referred to the "grapevine telegraph," a natural, twisted, and gnarled means of communication that worked through word-of-mouth. It seems that the phrase "grapevine telegraph" was first used to describe the communication network between slaves in the South, later spreading to more general use among soldiers in the Civil War. (Versions of this phrase appeared in other parts of the world as well, like Australia's "bush telegraph.")

The grapevine telegraph, though marveled at for its speed, was never considered to be a source of reliable information. In fact, in the late nineteenth century, newspapers accused their rivals of printing faulty information and unfounded rumors, claiming that they got their information not from the electrical telegraph, but from the grapevine version.

Of course, nowadays those same newspapers would probably lift the rumor, post it on their Web site, and call it an exclusive.

Q Why are bad moods called "the blues"?

A "The blues" are an abbreviation for the "blue devils." These pesky little demons, popularly believed to bring despondency and sadness, have been haunting minds since at least 1616. One of the first references to them was in *Times' Whistle,* a collection of satirical poems that was published that year: "Alston, whose life hath been accounted evill, And therfore cal'de by many the blew devill."

The glossary for that work contains the following entry for "Devil, blew devill": "'Blue devils,' the 'horrors,' or the remorse which frequently follows an ill course of life." Of course, an ill course of life is what usually transpires when one goes on a few too many benders. (Not that anyone on the F.Y.I. staff would know this in a firsthand way.)

According to John Russell Bartlett's *Dictionary of Americanisms* (1848), "blue was" once a common word in the habitual drinker's lexicon—it was a synonym for "drunk." Interestingly, Bartlett's dictionary also notes that "to have the blue devils is to be dispirited."

Now, you can take "dispirited" to mean "disheartened," "discouraged," "dejected," or "depressed." Or it could mean that someone got wise to your boozehound habits and cleared your cupboards of all spirits (i.e., whiskey, brandy, gin, and rum).

Many early sources, including the 1913 edition of *Webster's Revised Unabridged Dictionary,* define "blue devils" as "apparitions supposed to be seen by persons suffering with delirium tremens; hence, very low spirits." "Delirium tremens" are also known as "the d.t.'s," "the shakes," "seeing pink elephants," or the fevers that creep in during alcohol withdrawal.

Despite the somewhat demonic and alcohol-based origins of the blues, you certainly don't have to be a lush to come down with a case of them. These days, you've got plenty of reasons to have the blues: global warming, a sputtering economy. Or as Ella Fitzgerald sang, you can get the blues because your "ever-loving baby left town."

But it's not all doom and gloom if you're suffering from a particularly nasty case of the blues—they make really good antidepressants now.

Q What's so holy about Toledo, mackerel, smoke, or cows?

A The origins of these holy expressions are shrouded in mystery, myth, and perhaps a bit of absurdity. Whether we're talking about Toledo, mackerel, smoke, or cows, the only thing that etymologists can agree on is that the words are used as a type of euphemism known as a "minced oath" (an expletive without the expletive, if you will).

We'll tackle Toledo first—there are a couple of theories to explain how the phrase "holy Toledo" came to be. Etymologists tend to believe that it refers to the city of Toledo, Spain, whose thirteenth-century cathedral is one of the great Christian landmarks in Europe, as well as the place where the Archbishop of Spain does his Lord's work.

Not surprisingly, the unremarkable city of Toledo, Ohio, also claims to be the inspiration for this holy phrase. According to the Greater Toledo Convention and Visitors Bureau (GTCVB)—perhaps one of the least necessary organizations in existence—"holy

Toledo" just might refer to the large number of churches in the city. Or, as the GTCVB also suggests, the phrase might have originated with the famous preacher Billy Sunday, who supposedly called Toledo holy during a 1911 sermon. Both of these theories seem to border on the ridiculous, but we have to give the GTCVB an "A" for effort.

On to "holy mackerel." When one thinks of sanctified fish, Catholics spring to mind; traditionally, they've eaten fish on Fridays during lent. According to the research folks over at *Merriam-Webster,* the oath—which may have been a mockery of "holy Michael" or "holy Mary"—seems to have originated in the United States in the early nineteenth century, when American antipathy toward Roman Catholics was high. Apparently, insults were a little more civilized in those days.

As for "holy smoke," one common explanation holds that it refers to the puffs of smoke that the Vatican releases when a new pope has been selected. Regardless, the phrase was first used in print as an exclamation by Rudyard Kipling in 1892, when he wrote, "By the holy smoke, some one has got to urge girls to stand by the old machine." No, our crack F.Y.I. staff has no idea what it means, either.

"Holy cow" is a favorite among baseball fans, particularly those who follow the Chicago Cubs. The team's late broadcaster, Harry Caray, made the phrase famous, but it's actually been around since the turn of the twentieth century. Where it came from is (not surprisingly) a subject of debate, but etymologists believe that "holy cow" may refer to those genuine holy cows of India, considered sacred by religious tradition. And all this time, we thought a holy cow equaled a home run.

Q How can people get into a pickle?

A Well, you'd need a really big pickle—or you'd need to be a really small person. In either case, if you tried literally to get into a pickle, you would find yourself in a pickle of the metaphorical sort, whether you had succeeded or not. Got that? In the non-literal sense, to be in a pickle is to be in a quandary or a troubling situation of some kind. It's obvious that anyone who tried to actually get inside of a pickle would be in a serious mess. But what kind of nut would think of doing this in the first place?

The answer lies in the history of the language. Today when we think of a pickle, we imagine a cucumber that has been soaked in a savory brine—delicious, perhaps, but not much more than a garnish. But before the advent of refrigeration, pickling wasn't just for otherwise tasteless vegetables—it was a way of life. The process creates an acidic environment that kills the microorganisms that destroy fresh food; pickling, then, was an easy way to store scarce food for long periods of time. Before the invention of modern preservation techniques, it was extremely popular to pickle almost anything that was edible, from vegetables to fruit to pieces of meat.

The phrase "in a pickle" goes back hundreds of years to the heyday of pickling. At that time, the word "pickle" referred not only to the pickled food, but also to the pickling solution itself. In fact, "pickle" comes from the Old Dutch word *pekel* ("brine"). And to be in a pickle was to be in the brine—a state of affairs that would have delicious results for a cucumber, but a less pleasant effect on a person. Anyone who has gazed wonderingly at a jar of pickled pigs' feet has an idea of the ultimate consequences.

How old is the idea of being in a pickle? Old enough to have been used by Shakespeare—in fact, he was the first to publish the phrase. In *The Tempest,* Trinculo says to Alonso, "I have been in such a pickle since I saw you last that, I fear me, will never out of my bones: I shall not fear fly-blowing."

We're not sure what kind of freaky stuff Trinculo had in mind, but that's one pickle we're not into.

Q What do gin and rum have to do with gin rummy?

A Remember those childhood visits to some ancient relative's house? The adults talked of people you didn't know, the television didn't have cable, and the evening inevitably included a really weird card game in which the players knocked on the table.

What the grown-ups were playing was gin rummy. Simplified, the rules call for each player to be dealt ten cards with the goal of making "melds." That's a term for sets of three or more cards in series (consecutive numbers of the same suit) or matches (three of a kind, for example). The players draw and discard, trying to arrange their hands so that all the cards are melded. When a player thinks he or she has a winning hand, he or she "knocks" on the table, indicating the last round of play.

It's widely thought that the game originated in Mexico and came to the United States through Texas in the nineteenth century. Rummy, this theory holds, has roots in a Latin American game known as *conquain*. Bastardized by English speakers as "coon can," *conquain* shares much with gin rummy, including the knocking. Some historians, however, say that rummy owes more to the Chinese game *kun p'ai,* a cousin of mah-jongg.

Regardless, most scholars agree that the version played at your grandparents' house was developed in 1909 by Elwood and C. G. Baker, a father-son duo from Brooklyn. By the 1940s, their game was all the rage, thanks largely to its enormous popularity in Hollywood.

As for the name "gin rummy," the sleuths are stumped. Speculation abounds, from the popularity of gin and rum at the start of the twentieth century, to derivations of the card games *chinchón* from Spain or *kon khin* from China. We're fond of the theory that when Elwood Baker developed a new rummy game, he chose the name "gin" as a play on "rummy." Now that you're old enough, feel free to knock a few back in Elwood's honor.

Chapter Twelve

MORE GOOD STUFF

Q Why do parents give their kids names that no one can pronounce or spell?

A For many years, we've relied upon celebrities to give their children the types of bizarre names that leave the rest of us scratching our heads. Examples abound—from Frank Zappa's kids Moon Unit and Dweezil to Lisa Bonet's son Nakoa-Wolf Manakauapo Namakaeha Momoa. But much like tattoos and body piercings, funny-sounding baby names aren't just for celebrities anymore.

Names have always been subjected to the ever-shifting whims of fashion, although the most popular monikers for boys remain more stable than those for girls. According to the Social Security

Administration, Michael ranked as the top name for boys from 1961 to 1998; Jacob ascended to the top spot in 1999 and maintained it through 2007. During that same period, Mary, Lisa, Jennifer, Jessica, Ashley, and Emily all spent time atop the girls' chart.

But recent trends have changed the game—not the names themselves, but the way they're chosen. In 1880, 41 percent of boys and 23 percent of girls were given names that were among their gender's ten most popular; by 2006, those figures had fallen to 9.5 percent for boys and 8 percent for girls. Modern parents want their children's names to be unique, for a variety of reasons.

A mother who named her daughter Jennifer in 1975 surely knew that she was choosing a popular name, but she didn't have the resources to obsess about it—there are only so many books of baby names in the library, after all. But the mother of today has a vast sea of knowledge right at her fingertips; five minutes of Googling will reveal that her personal list of potential names is much less distinctive than she had hoped. In 2008, this realization led one Kansas couple to eschew tradition entirely, naming its daughter Gaea Althea Emma Ana Margherita VII Kaos.

Then there's the corporate-branding approach, which is supposedly a way to differentiate your offspring in the marketplace, giving them a competitive advantage over their more boringly named peers. Names chosen this way aren't hard to pronounce or spell, but they're still plenty weird. A professional baby-name consultant (yes, this is an actual occupation) told *The Wall Street Journal* that he named his son Beckett because the "C-K sound is very well regarded in corporate circles." (We here at F.Y.I. headquarters are all a little worried for young Beckett.)

But if all parents want to give their children unique names, it will create a paradox—having a one-of-a-kind name will eventually become as common and mundane as leftover tuna casserole on a Tuesday night. When everyone has a different name, no one's name will stand out. Which means that when it comes time for Gaea Althea Emma Ana Margherita VII Kaos to follow in her parents' footsteps and give her children the wildest, most unusual names she can think of, she'll probably choose Michael and Mary.

Q Is there anything new under the sun?

A It's right there in the Old Testament, in black and white. Ecclesiastes 1:9: "What has been will be again, what has been done will be done again; there is nothing new under the sun." Who's going to argue with the Bible?

Young people will: the enthralled young lovers who assume that nobody could possibly understand how they feel; the fiery young writers, artists, and musicians who strive nobly for nothing short of absolute originality; the eager, impassioned young soldiers who earnestly go off to fight a war to end all wars. With age and experience, however, comes the realization that everybody falls in love, every story has been told, and history repeats itself with the same bloody, humbling results.

Ecclesiastes recounts Solomon's search for meaning in life. Is there anything new under the sun? Solomon says no. He could not have foreseen nuclear weapons, Google, space travel, heart transplants, or the Chia Pet. But Solomon wasn't concerned with material things—he was searching for meaning. And he found none. No matter who we are and what we do, no matter how good or bad we are, we all share the same fate: certain death.

Pretty bleak, huh? Not necessarily. Ecclesiastes 9:9–10 also includes this: "Enjoy life with your wife, whom you love, all the days of this meaningless life that God has given you under the sun—all your meaningless days. For this is your lot in life and in your toilsome labor under the sun. Whatever your hand finds to do, do it with all your might, for in the grave, where you are going, there is neither working nor planning nor knowledge nor wisdom." In other words, you only get one chance, so always live life to the fullest. It's now or never: Be good, do your best, and love your family and friends.

Okay, now that we F.Y.I. staffers have revealed the meaning of life, we'll promptly return to the fart jokes and cultural curiosities.

Q Do actions really speak louder than words?

A Mark Twain said, "Action speaks louder than words, but not nearly as often." Sure, what you do means more than what you say. But guess what? Most people—particularly politicians—are much better at talking the talk than walking the walk.

Just think of all the verbal promises we break on a daily basis: "Yes, Mom, I'll take out the garbage." "Yes, dear, I'll be home for dinner at six." "Yes, sir! That report will be on your desk first thing tomorrow morning."

Heck, what about all of the pacts that we make with ourselves that we wind up breaking? Chances are, every January 1 you're saying things to yourself like: *I will join the gym . . . I will join a book club . . . I will be a better person . . . I will eat my veggies . . . I will quit smoking . . . I will drink milk . . . I will go to church . . . I will save more money . . . I will save the world.*

Did you do what you said? Eh. That would have taken way too much effort. And that's just it. Actions speak louder than words because they take commitment and determination to complete. No wonder we're so impressed with people who run marathons, join the Peace Corps, or just manage to make it to work on time every day. They actually get up off their butts.

It's real easy to talk about something but much harder to actually do it. And it seems this truth is universal. Do actions really speak louder than words? Conventional wisdom certainly tells us so. Versions of the expression "actions speak louder than words" can be found across many languages and cultures, dating back to ancient Greece. In the fourth century BC, Athenian philosopher Demosthenes (the greatest public speaker of antiquity) said: "All speech is vain and empty unless it be accompanied by action." In other words, talk is cheap.

Q What's the point of multiple life sentences?

A No, the justice system isn't secretly Buddhist. There are good reasons for multiple life sentences, and they don't have anything to do with reincarnation.

Logically enough, judges hand down multiple sentences to go along with multiple criminal offenses. Multiple charges may be decided in the same trial, but they are still considered separate crimes and often yield separate punishments. Even in the case of life imprisonment, multiple sentences can end up being very important in the rare cases in which convictions are overturned on appeals.

Let's say a jury finds a man guilty of killing five people. The judge might sentence him to five life sentences to go along with the five charges. Even if any one of the convictions is overturned (or even if four of them are overturned), the murderer still has to carry out a life sentence. To walk free, he would have to be exonerated of all five murders.

Furthermore, "life" doesn't always mean an entire lifetime. Depending on the sentencing guidelines of the state, the judge may sentence a man to life imprisonment with the possibility of parole. In this instance, life is the maximum length of the sentence, meaning that the defendant could conceivably go free if a parole board releases him after he's served the minimum time (thirty years, for example).

If, however, a defendant is convicted on multiple charges, the judge may hand down multiple life sentences with the possibility of parole—but the judge can also specify that those sentences are to be served consecutively rather than concurrently. This way the prisoner will not get a parole hearing until the minimum time for all the sentences put together has been served.

Consider multiple life sentences to be a safeguard, a way to ensure that the bad guys never see the light of day.

Q What's the longest earthworm on record?

A In 1967 someone near King William's Town, South Africa, found a twenty-two-foot-long African giant earthworm, or *Microchaetus rappi,* by the roadside. Lost to history, unfortunately, are some key facts, such as who exactly found it, what the worm was doing there, and whether it was alive. But the editors of *Earth Worm Digest*—whose stated mission is "to disseminate earthworm information in a responsible way"—accept this anecdote as true, so we'll say that this is the longest earthworm on record.

The average *Microchaetus rappi* grows to a "mere" six or seven feet when stretched out. One runner-up among *annelids* (also known as segmented worms) is the giant Gippsland earthworm, *Megascolides australis,* which averages around three feet but can reach lengths of more than nine feet. Nearly extinct, it's found only in the Victoria region on the southwest tip of Australia. The people there think so highly of their giant worms that they've established the Giant Worm Museum in the town of Bass to educate the public about this endangered species. The River Mekong earthworm, *Megascolex (Promegascolex) mekongianus,* of Southeast Asia is another contender in the giant earthworm category. Similar to the Gippsland, it can measure up to nine feet long, and it has as many as five hundred or more individual body segments.

The United States has some mammoth earthworms in the Pacific Northwest. The Palouse earthworm averages around three feet long—small by the standards of Africa and Australia but certainly no midget by the standards of backyard gardeners. Discovered in 1897, it is so rarely seen that, by the end of the twentieth century, naturalists believed that it had become extinct. Then in 2005, University of Idaho grad student Yaniria Sanchez-de Leon uncovered one on the Idaho-Washington state border. Although her specimen was only six inches long, lab studies confirmed that it was a baby Palouse.

This discovery inspired Dr. Sam James, a biologist from the University of Kansas Natural History Museum, to persevere in his search for the *Rhinodrilus fafner,* an earthworm that can grow up to about six feet long and was last spotted in the Brazilian rainforest. Although his quarry was officially declared extinct in 2003, James is optimistic that it still exists. "Our position on these extinctions is that they are more likely to be off the radar than off the planet," he told the *New York Times* in 2007. Meanwhile, the African giant earthworm remains off the charts—the undisputed champion of the world.

Q Is "spotted dick" what it sounds like?

A Face it: Nobody visits England for the cuisine. From toad-in-the-hole to kidney pie, the British gustatory landscape is littered with dishes that sound disgusting and taste worse. But if you're in England, you have to eat *something.* And afterwards, you'll need to cleanse your palate. You could drink yet another pint (it's what the locals do, after all), but why not indulge in something different? Why not try some spotted dick?

Yes, spotted dick is a dessert—a pudding, to be precise. This is perhaps not surprising, considering that England is a land of puddings. In fact, in addition to brutal imperial slaughter, tea-drinking ninnies, and Monty Python, England may be best known as a country of pudding heads. Blood pudding, rice pudding, Cumberland pudding, Newcastle pudding, and Newmarket pudding. Then there's spotted dick, a suet pudding that is studded with raisins and currants. But why not simply call it spotted pudding? Must we refer to it as dick?

Nobody is quite sure why Brits started calling one of their most traditional dishes by such an unpalatable name. Looking at a traditional spotted dick—which is essentially a steamed log of suet—the answer may seem obvious. But apparently, the obvious answer isn't good enough for etymologists and their fancy research methods.

One unlikely theory suggest that the name came from the dish's supposed resemblance to a spotted dog (in the nineteenth century, dogs were often named Dick). Other word sleuths contend that "dick" is a bastardization of "dough," which also makes little to no sense.

Most etymologists believe that the phrase may have evolved as a corruption of "dink," which, in turn, was short for "puddink" (itself a bastardization of "pudding"). Why none of the other forty-two thousand puddings on the British menu are known by this moniker remains a bit of a mystery.

Despite its venerable status in England, times change. In 2001, baffled by the plummeting sales of the pudding, the British supermarket chain Tesco sponsored a survey of shoppers. The leading response by far was that they were too embarrassed to ask for spotted dick by name. Though marketing gurus considered changing the name, tradition won the day, and the product continues to be sold under the spotted dick moniker.

Nevertheless, spotted dick may be headed the way of the Lesser Bilby. According to market surveys, spotted dick's popularity is dwindling at such a rapid clip that by 2021, it may be completely wiped off the British culinary map (as desolate, and absurd, as it already is).

Q Why are bike models different for boys and girls?

A Frankly, the whole thing is kind of weird. On a boy's bicycle, the top tube that stretches from the handlebars to the seat is straight; on a girl's model, it's at an angle, leaving some empty space right in front of the seat. As any guy who's hit the brakes and slid off the seat knows all too well, the straight top tube and the male anatomy aren't exactly compatible. Shouldn't males be riding the female version? What's the deal?

As you might have already deduced, pioneering bike makers of the 1880s didn't have physiology in mind. Their reasoning was that a straight top tube made for a sturdier frame. And the female design? When women's frames were introduced around 1890, bike manufacturers came up with this variation in order to maintain a sense of decorum on the streets and sidewalks. Back then, women wore dresses or skirts for just about everything, including biking around town. Angling the top tube made it easier for a lady to mount and ride a bike without exposing her intimate undergarments. (Those cursed bike makers!)

You don't see many women cycling in long skirts these days, so there's really no point to the varying designs. Some manufacturers still make the classic female bike, though mostly for kids. Serious female cyclists typically ride bikes with straight top tubes.

As for the guys? If they're worried about slamming their equipment into their equipment, they can always purchase a classic girl's bike. It's a matter of whether they prefer to put their manhood at risk literally or figuratively.

Q Whatever happened to the family station wagon?

A Video may have killed the radio star, but it was the minivan that killed the family wagon. Funny how advanced technology has a way of eradicating the things that you love the most. But, hey, sometimes you don't know what you've got until it's gone—and that full-size two-tone Ford Country Squire with imitation wood paneling has long since left the highway for that big rest stop in the sky.

How did it get there? Back in the 1960s and 1970s, the station wagon was the ultimate symbol of suburbia. It seemed that every growing family—even the fictional ones—had one. Steve Douglas (of *My Three Sons*) drove a Pontiac

Bonneville, Lucy and Ricky got a Ford, and the Bradys packed the whole bunch into a Plymouth Satellite and took a road trip to the Grand Canyon.

Eventually, the kids who lived in the heyday of the family wagon grew up and started families of their own. And guess what? They'd rather die than be seen in one of those tacky tot-toting land barges that their moms and dads used to drive.

So when Chrysler introduced the first minivan in 1983, it became a hit. Other car manufacturers quickly rushed their own models to market, and the "practical" family-friendly minivan poached wagon sales to the point that domestic carmakers lost interest in making them.

Many car experts believe that the final nail was put in the wagon's coffin when Ford introduced the Explorer in 1990. It looked a lot like a station wagon, but Ford knew better than to call it one. The SUV was born, and according Tom Magliozzi, host of National Public Radio's *Car Talk,* the family station wagon was effectively replaced: "Men didn't think it was cool to drive their families around in station wagons. But the car makers discovered that if you raised them a little higher, put big, fat tires on them, and slapped four-by-four decals on the back, men would fall all over themselves to drive them."

Today's kids will never know the joy of side-facing bench seats (or riding "freestyle" in the back cargo space of a full-size Vista Cruiser with no seats at all). But they're probably too busy watching SpongeBob SquarePants DVDs on their factory-installed minivan entertainment systems to really think about what they're missing.

Q Is marrying a Siamese twin considered bigamy?

A Even before P. T. Barnum hired the "Siamese Twins"—Chang and Eng Bunker—and carted them around the world as part of his freak show, conjoined twins had captured a place in the public imagination. And the curiosity over them continues today. Not the least of the intrigues are the ethical and legal questions that are raised when two people share parts of the same body. If one twin commits murder against the other's wishes, does one get punished unfairly or does the other get off scot-free? What happens when they show up on two-for-one day at Six Flags? And if you marry one of the twins, would you be arrested for bigamy?

We don't know how Six Flags would see it, but we do know that, according to modern law, conjoined twins are considered two individuals with separate identities and rights. This means that, in most cases, marrying a Siamese twin wouldn't result in bigamy charges—unless you tried to marry both of them. But it's a tricky call because there isn't much in the way of precedent.

For much of history, conjoined twins were considered "monsters" that were deformed by God's wrath or the Devil's mischief. Some were sideshow curiosities—indeed, many pairs of conjoined twins made handsome livings exhibiting themselves in halls and theaters around the world. Besides Barnum's original "Siamese Twins," there were the "Two-Headed Nightingale," the "Blended Tocci Brothers," and Violet and Daisy Hilton, the most famous conjoined twins of the twentieth century.

The Hiltons—no relation to the contemporary freak-show Hiltons—were showbiz stars who made two films, the 1932 hit

Freaks and the 1951 bomb *Chained for Life.* The Hiltons also tested the legality of conjoined-twin marriage when, in 1934, Violet Hilton and her bandleader, Maurice L. Lambert, applied for a marriage license in Manhattan. The city clerk refused, calling such a request "immoral." When Violet (and Daisy) and Maurice fled to New Jersey to seek a license there, the Newark clerk also refused on moral grounds. Eventually Violet's petition was refused by no fewer than twenty-one states, effectively ending her engagement to Lambert.

Interestingly, one of the reasons cited for the license refusals was that Daisy was not engaged. This was not a problem for P. T. Barnum's twins, Chang and Eng, who settled down with a couple of North Carolina sisters, with whom the brothers combined to sire twenty-one children (which raises another question that we'll let somebody else answer).

Nowadays, of course, conjoined twins aren't sideshow curiosities; they're individuals with the same rights and responsibilities of every other citizen. But before we get too high and mighty about our enlightened modern sensibilities, consider that in 2003 the Farrelly brothers put out *Stuck on You,* a truly abysmal movie about conjoined twins. The film grossed nearly seventy million dollars. Talk about a sucker being born every minute.

Q Why are guinea pigs used in so many experiments?

A Why do guinea pigs make such good, well, guinea pigs? The answer is simple: Even though these furry little creatures don't look like us, they have some very human physiological features.

Like humans, guinea pigs, or *Cavia porcellus,* are among the few mammals that can't synthesize their own vitamin C, and they have significant dietary requirements for potassium, folic acid, and thiamine; these traits make them useful for studies on nutrition. In addition, they're susceptible to many of the infectious diseases that plague humans. Research using guinea pigs has contributed to cures for tuberculosis, diphtheria, yellow fever, cholera, pneumonia, and several strains of typhus.

A guinea pig also has an immune system that is similar to ours, and the animals is prone to the same allergies. Guinea pigs readily succumb to anaphylactic shock, an extreme allergic reaction that can cause death if it's not treated immediately. Because of this, they have been instrumental to the development of the inhalers and other oral medications that human asthmatics rely on to breathe freely.

Guinea pig ears are set up like ours, too, which enables scientists to study ways of reducing deafness. In 1961, Georg von Békésy of Hungary won the Nobel Prize in the medical field for his pioneering research on the function of the cochlea, the inner part of the ear, using—you guessed it—guinea pigs as his initial subjects.

According to Simon Festing, director of Britain's Research Defence Society, guinea pig research has led to twenty-three Nobel prizes in medicine or physiology. You'd think that research labs would be overflowing with the critters, but guinea pigs account for only 20 percent of all lab animals in the United States and just 1.7 percent in Britain.

People who are opposed to animal research believe that guinea pigs shouldn't be in labs at all. If you're uncomfortable with the idea of animal experimentation, you'll be glad to know that veterinarian Viktor Reinhardt, lab-animal advisor to the Animal Welfare Institute of Washington, D.C., has issued a series of guidelines, "Comfortable Quarters for Guinea-Pigs in Research Institutions," for government and university researchers. Guinea pigs, it turns out, share not just some of our physical traits, but also many of our emotional ones. In order to enjoy happy (albeit short) lives, guinea pigs require environments where they can socialize with each other. And when three's a crowd, they need quiet places to get away from it all, just like most of us do.

Outside of the lab, guinea pigs are popular pets. So on the whole, the guinea pig population of the planet is healthy and well—and thanks to these little animals, millions of people are, too.

Q Why isn't acting in pornography considered prostitution?

A Or we could put it this way: If having sex for money is legal when you're making pornography, why don't johns just bring along video cameras when they hire prostitutes? In the eyes of the law, the camera is significant, but putting the deed on tape isn't what makes the difference. The distinction between pornography and prostitution comes down to who's paying whom for what.

In the United States, prostitution is largely regulated by the states. Aside from Rhode Island and Nevada, all states prohibit it completely—but they define and punish it differently. In California, where most American porn is made, the law states that prostitution occurs when someone pays another person for gratification through sexual contact. The crime isn't exactly the exchange of money for sex—the gratification part is what gets people into hot water. In pornography, the actors and actresses are paid to have sex, but they're not paid to gratify each other or, for that matter, the producer who's paying them. And if they happen to actually gratify each other in the process of *acting* gratified? Well, it's not illegal, since they didn't have to do it to get paid.

And what about the porn consumers, who are most certainly paying money for DVDs that they'll use in the pursuit of some solo gratification? That's not illegal, either. Apparently these dirty DVDs have "serious literary, artistic, political, or scientific value," as the California Supreme Court put it, which means that they're protected as free speech under the First Amendment.

This was the basic reasoning in the most significant ruling regarding the porn/prostitution question, the California Supreme Court's 1988 decision in *People v. Freeman*. A lower court convicted Harold Freeman of procuring somebody for the purpose of prostitution, a felony under the state's pandering laws, as part of his work producing the porn classic *Caught from Behind, Part II*. The California Supreme Court ruled that Freeman was not guilty since there was no evidence that he was paying the actors for his or their sexual gratification. Instead, he was paying them to appear in a movie, which is protected by the First Amendment.

This legal precedent gave the porn industry in California license to make all the dirty movies it pleased. It also made prosecutors in other states wary of using the same legal tactic: Lose the case, and a precedent could be set that makes your state a haven for pornographers. And before long, *Caught From Behind, Part IX* might begin filming in the shadow of your state capitol building.

Q Where is the original skid row?

A Fans of 1980s hair bands have been asking this question for nearly two decades. After exploding onto the rock scene in 1989 with an eponymous powerhouse album—featuring such anthems as "Youth Gone Wild" and the quintessential power ballad "I Remember You"—Skid Row vanished from the public eye a few years later. Whatever happened to Sebastian Bach? What about Snake Sabo? Wait, what's that? You're not asking about the rock band? You say that you're interested in where the phrase "skid row" originated? Well, that certainly is disappointing—we'd already put on our acid-washed jeans and thrust our lighters into the air. But we suppose we can answer that question, too.

"Skid row," a term used to describe a section of an urban community that is inhabited by the poor and down-on-their-luck, has been around since the Great Depression. A variation of the phrase goes back even further, to around 1880. In the Pacific Northwest in the late nineteenth century, logging was a booming business, and getting the timber from the remote mountainsides to lumber mills was no easy task, especially in the rainy conditions that companies often had to work.

To facilitate transportation, lumbermen placed timbers—which were known as "skids"—over the unpaved logging trails. They then dragged the felled logs over these timber-covered logging trails, which became known as "skid roads." (Incidentally, two other phrases are spawned from this practice: "on the skids" and "grease the skids.")

Where the first skid road originated is up for debate—a number of Pacific Northwest cities lay claim to it, including Seattle, where a Skid Road still exists—but it wasn't long before the term was used to describe the parts of town where these hardworking lumbermen lived and would gather on their days off to carouse and behave badly. These questionable parts of the city, which were often filled with saloons and houses of ill repute, also drew the unemployed and others who were down on their luck. Over the next few decades, the term skid road morphed into skid row and spread across the country with the tramps and vagabonds who rode box-cars from city to city.

By the Great Depression, millions of Americans had joined the ranks of the down-and-out, and skid rows popped up in cities across the nation. Nowadays, people don't use the phrase quite as often. In fact, you'd be hard-pressed to find somebody who could direct you to skid row in any modern city. Although if you're look-ing for the members of the once-great band of the same name, it might be a good place to look.

Q Why do women get bitchy when they are about to have their period?

A Guys should consider rephrasing this question before they ask it to a woman. Trust us.

Premenstrual Syndrome (PMS) was established as an official medical condition in 1931. Symptoms usually manifest one to two weeks before a woman menstruates and can last for the entire period. The physical symptoms include headaches, aching joints, bloating, and fatigue; the psychological symptoms include irritability, anxiety, and insomnia.

Eighty to 90 percent of women experience some of these symptoms to varying degrees and in various combinations. PMS typically involves discomfort, but this doesn't interfere with a woman's ability to go about her daily routine. However, for 20 to 40 percent of women, the symptoms are severe enough to disrupt their lives. A hormone-related migraine, for example, might prevent a woman from going to work, and irritability might adversely affect her relationships.

The worst PMS sufferers are diagnosed with Premenstrual Dysphoric Disorder (PMDD). This affliction, caused by the biological and hormonal effects of PMS, affects 3 to 8 percent of women. PMDD causes irritability, depression, and physical issues that severely disrupt a woman's ability to function.

PMS is caused by a change in the levels of hormones—most notably progesterone and estrogen—during the normal menstrual cycle. But there is hope: A healthy diet and regular exercise can decrease the symptoms in many women, and over-the-counter medications also can be effective.

As for the guys, here's one last word of advice: If you know your girlfriend's or wife's "time of the month" is nearing, proceed with extreme caution. It will be better for everyone involved. Again, trust us.

Q How do you hypnotize someone?

A A hypnotist in a show at a Las Vegas casino might employ a flourish of mystical words and fancy moves to mesmerize volunteers, but it's all for show. The real way to hypnotize someone is much simpler and doesn't require a swinging pocket watch or a lovely sequined assistant.

Psychologists don't fully understand hypnosis, but they generally agree that it's a relaxed, hyper-attentive trance, similar to daydreaming. The defining quality of this state is that subjects don't scrutinize and interpret information as they normally would. When a hypnotist makes a suggestion ("Your hands feel heavy, very heavy"), the subject processes the information as if it was real.

A hypnotist induces this trance by getting a subject to relax fully and focus his or her attention on something. This can be as simple as asking the subject to stare at a blank Post-it note for fifteen minutes or so while saying in a soothing voice that the subject is feeling sleepy and his or her eyelids are getting heavy. Generally, the hypnotist reads from a script or recites memorized lines that help the subject to relax different parts of the body and to imagine a carefree state of mind.

Once the subject is in a trance, the hypnotist can make all sorts of suggestions. How exactly does this work? The hypnotist "programs" specific reactions into the subject—such as, "When I snap my fingers, you will start speaking in gibberish and then you will put a lampshade on your head"—that will be enacted when he or she is summoned from the trance.

Hypnotism doesn't work on everyone. About 10 to 15 percent of the adult population is highly susceptible to it, meaning that these people enter hypnosis easily and respond to many different types of hypnotic suggestions; about 10 percent can't be hypnotized; and the balance of people can be hypnotized but respond in only limited ways to the suggestions. For example, moderately hypnotizable people usually won't follow a suggestion to forget the hypnosis session, whereas the highly hypnotizable will.

For those who are highly suggestible, hypnosis can be an excellent therapeutic tool. It's been effective in reducing nausea from chemotherapy, labor pain, and general anxiety. And if you want to see your friend strut around clucking like a chicken, it can't be beat.

Q Do figure skaters get dizzy after fast spins?

A Some skaters say that they do get dizzy; others swear that they don't. But they all agree on one important point: Practice diminishes dizziness. That's hardly a scientific answer—remember, we're talking about people who wear sequins for a living—but it does have some credibility.

Dizziness is usually caused by a temporary malfunction of something called the vestibular system, an amazing set of tiny membranes and channels in your inner ear. This organ system senses the motion and orientation of your head, primarily with a group of three semicircular canals that each register movement in a different direction. These canals contain fluid, and as this fluid shifts with the movements of your head, your brain receives feedback so that it can compensate for the motion.

When you spin, you play tricks on your vestibular system. If the fluid in those semicircular canals gets moving fast enough, it can't respond immediately when you stop. Because the fluid stays in motion for a while, it sends a message that your head is moving even after it has stopped. Your brain believes this misguided message and continues to make adjustments to compensate for this nonexistent motion. That's why your eyes feel like they're spinning in your head, and why keeping your balance and walking a straight line are difficult or impossible.

When doctors work with patients who are having problems with balance or dizziness, one therapy they recommend is vestibular rehabilitation, in which the patient undertakes a regime of head and eye movements designed to recreate whatever conditions are causing the dizziness. The goal is to repeatedly reach that threshold of dizziness and train the brain to compensate for it.

Skaters do the same thing when they practice spins over and over again. They train their brains to grow accustomed to spinning, and their recovery time from dizziness grows shorter and shorter. This, of course, allows them more time to conjure those persistent fake grins that they wear for the television cameras as their disappointing scores are given.

Q Who opened the first restaurant?

A This question has produced a wide range of answers among researchers. One group points to the 1760s in Paris, where Mathurin Roze de Chantoiseau offered a hearty soup stock that was thought to restore health by delivering all the goodness of meat and vegetables without the putative digestive "risks" of solid food. The first restaurant that followed the current format of customers sitting at individual tables and eating portions of food that they chose from a menu—rather than a dish that was dictated that day by a cook—during set hours of operation is thought to have opened in 1782, thanks to Antoine Beauvilliers, also a Parisian.

But there's something quaint about the effort to affix the "first" label to these spots, and something that smacks of Western bias. Presumably, these eating places are the beginning of the lineage that extends to our American restaurants today. But how can you say with certainty that an idea as basic as the restaurant originated in any one place and at any one time?

Folks have been eating at dedicated dining establishments for more than a thousand years. It's conceivable that restaurant-like establishments existed in ancient Greece, ancient Rome, and the Near or Far East long before the French were claiming that their stew broth was good for people with "weakness of chest." A spot in China whose name translates to "Ma Yu Ching's Bucket Chicken House" (no kidding) was established more than 850 years ago and is still operating.

Enough said. If you want to know the direct link to our American eateries, look to pre-revolutionary Paris. But if you want to know the earliest actual restaurants, you need to go back a lot further. The fact is, people have always loved having someone else cook for them.

CONTRIBUTORS

Tom Harris is a Web project consultant, editor, and writer living in Atlanta. He is the co-founder of Explainist.com, and was leader of the editorial content team at HowStuffWorks.com.

Jack Greer is a writer living in Chicago.

Anthony G. Craine is a contributor to the *Britannica Book of the Year* and has written for magazines including *Inside Sports* and *Ask.* He is a former United Press International bureau chief.

Diane Lanzillotta Bobis is a food, fashion, and lifestyle writer from Glenview, Illinois.

Pat Sherman is a writer living in Cambridge, Massachusetts. She is the author several books for children, including *The Sun's Daughter* and *Ben and the Proclamation of Emancipation.*

Noah Liberman is a Chicago-based sports, entertainment, and business writer who has published two books and has contributed articles to a wide range of newspapers and national magazines.

Alex Nechas is a writer and editor living in Chicago.

Joshua D. Boeringa is a writer living in Mt. Pleasant, Michigan. He has written for magazines and Web sites.

Matt Clark is a writer living in Brooklyn, Ohio.

Paul Forrester is an editor living in New York City.

Vickey Kalambakal is a writer and historian based in Southern California. She writes for textbooks, encyclopedias, magazines, and ezines.

Carrie Williford is a writer living in Atlanta. She was a contributin writer to HowStuffWorks.com.

Letty Livingston is a dating coach, relationship counselor, and sexpert. Her advice column, Let Letty Help, has been published in more than forty periodicals and on the Internet (letlettyhelp. blogspot.com).

Jeff Moores is an illustrator whose work appears in periodicals and advertisements, and as licensed characters on clothing. Visit his website (jeffmoores.com) to see more of his work.

Factual verification: Darcy Chadwick, Barbara Cross, Bonny M. Davidson, Andrew Garrett, Cindy Hangartner, Brenda McLean, Carl Miller, Katrina O'Brien, Marilyn Perlberg